WAR ZONE
PANDORAX

959.M41

Contents

Written by: Jervis Johnson

Cover Art: Kevin Chin

Art, Design, Production and Reprographics
by the Games Workshop Design Studio

www.games-workshop.com

UK
Games Workshop Ltd,
Willow Rd, Lenton,
Nottingham,
NG7 2WS

NORTHERN EUROPE
Games Workshop Ltd,
Willow Rd, Lenton,
Nottingham,
NG7 2WS

NORTH AMERICA
Games Workshop Inc,
6211 East Holmes Road,
Memphis,
Tennessee 38141

AUSTRALIA
Games Workshop,
23 Liverpool Street,
Ingleburn,
NSW 2565

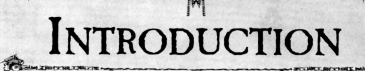

INTRODUCTION

All across the Imperium, massive campaigns are fought to control vital planets or annihilate hated enemies. These vast conflicts are so momentous that they shape history itself, as armies clash for years or even decades to secure victory.

Some of those campaigns have become synonymous with war on a scale unimaginable; planets whose names have become a litany of disaster – Armageddon, Medusa V, Damnos, Skalathrax, Terra itself – the list stretches into the annals of the Imperium for ten thousand years and more. Such campaigns turn the planets and systems where they are fought into ravaged war zones, where the only thing the battle-hardened inhabitants know is death and destruction.

This book describes the Pandorax War Zone, and the desperate battles that were fought there between a Chaos incursion force led by Abaddon the Despoiler, and the forces of the Imperium led by Dark Angels Commander Azrael. The campaign was fought all across the Pandorax System, both in the depths of space and upon the monster-infested surface of the death world known as Pythos, beneath the surface of which lay a dormant Warp portal known as the Damnation Cache. Abaddon managed to reactivate the Damnation Cache, and used it to unleash hordes of Daemons to overrun the planet. At the height of the campaign, Chaos Space Marines and Daemons battled against an Imperial force that included a massive Imperial Guard army, bolstered by the arrival of the entire Dark Angels Chapter and a brotherhood of Grey Knights.

APOCALYPSE WAR ZONES

Each Apocalypse War Zone is a self-contained supplement to the Apocalypse rules, based on a famous campaign from the history of the Warhammer 40,000 galaxy. Each War Zone starts off with a detailed history that describes the course of the campaign, the famous battles that were part of it, and the combatants that waged the war.

The background is followed by special rules, Strategic Assets, missions and Apocalypse Formations, all of which are based on the history and background of the War Zone. You can use all of these things when you fight a battle set in the War Zone, and with a little bit of common sense they can also be used for Apocalypse battles set in similar theatres of war elsewhere. It's worth noting that the War Zone Apocalypse Formations can be used in any Apocalypse battle that you fight, even those set elsewhere.

Last but not least, each Apocalypse War Zone includes a gatefold that unfolds to show a 'battle report' of an Apocalypse game set in that War Zone. We hope that it will serve as an example of what can be achieved with time and effort, and as an inspiration for the games of Apocalypse you take part in yourself.

THE PANDORAX INCURSION

The Pandorax Incursion took place between 959.M41 and 961.M41, when a Black Legion warfleet invaded the Pandorax System and captured the Imperial planet of Pythos. Hidden beneath the planet's surface was a portal to the Warp known as the Damnation Cache, which Abaddon used to unleash a daemonic legion upon the world. A ferocious campaign was fought by Imperial forces to recapture Pythos and close down the Damnation Cache, first in the depths of space, and then on the daemon-infested surface of Pythos itself.

THE INVASION OF PYTHOS

In 959.M41, a Black Legion incursion fleet invaded the Imperial planet of Pythos, in the Pandorax System. The fleet was commanded by Abaddon the Despoiler himself, and consisted of half a dozen massive battleships, each one with enough firepower to lay waste to an entire planet, supported by numerous escort craft.

The incursion fleet contemptuously swept aside Pandorax's system defence craft, and moved into orbit above the planet of Pythos within hours of entering the system. What Abaddon could possibly want from Pythos was by no means clear at this time. The planet was an inhospitable death

world, home to a colony of hardy Imperial citizens. Most of Pythos is covered in dense jungle, which is home to massive saurian creatures happy to eat anything that moves. The oceans are inhabited by equally large predators.

Because of the dangers of moving through the lowlands and across the oceans, the human settlers of Pythos settled in mountaintop mining colonies known locally as delver-strongholds. From these, they derived a precarious and meagre existence mining the precious minerals found in the planet's mountain chains. Hundreds of these strongholds were scattered over the planet, each home to populations of only a few thousand Imperial citizens.

SEPULTURE WASTES

MOUTH OF EREBRAX

HOLLOWFAL MOUNTAINS

PYXIS MOUNTAINS

PYTHOS PRIME

MOUNT OLYMPAX

HIVE ATIKA

HESODIKAS

THE DEATHGLADES

EYE OF EREBRAX

MAUSCOLCA PRIMUS

BELUOSUS

STRAITS OF ANNIHILATION

● MAJOR DELVER-STRONGHOLDS

● HIVE CITY

PYTHOS
IMPERIAL DEATH WORLD
Pythos is a death world, covered mainly in dense jungles, with occasional areas of scorched grassland. Its jungles and oceans are inhabited by massive saurian predators.

ABADDON THE DESPOILER

Abaddon took command of the Black Legion following the Horus Heresy and has led it in innumerable bloody campaigns since then. He secured the favour of all four of the Ruinous Powers, who have rewarded him with the arcane blade Drach'nyen, to use alongside the Talon of Horus, the legendary weapon of the Warmaster himself. With the Dark Gods behind him, Abaddon is determined to avenge Horus and destroy the Imperium. Should his armies triumph, a tide of Chaos will pour from the Eye of Terror to engulf the galaxy.

Pythos' only major city was the Hive-port of Atika, which was located on the coast of the planet's largest ocean, and surrounded on its landward side by the aptly named deathglades. Atika was a small spire city with its main habitation zones located in the dome-like upper levels of the city, high above the surrounding swamplands. Travel between Atika and the delver-strongholds was carried out in dilapidated lighter-than-air dirigibles known as sky barges, lumbering through the skies high above the ferocious creatures that inhabited the lowlands in relative safety.

This, then, was the bleak environment which Abaddon found at Pythos. Within moments of entering orbit, his warfleet unleashed a pinpoint barrage, quickly disabling Atika's defences and blasting the bastions and barracks occupied by the city's defence forces. Blood red rain started pouring from the skies, and the massive capital ships of the Chaos fleet launched scores of Dreadclaw drop pods, which disgorged hundreds of Chaos Space Marines. Dozens of squads of Khorne Berserkers supported by hunting packs of Forgefiends led the assault, slaughtering the defenders in a maelstrom of gore.

Surprised, demoralised, and having already suffered heavy casualties, Atika's defenders broke almost at first contact. The only formation able to organize any kind of effective resistance was the 183rd Catachan Jungle Fighter regiment, stranded on the planet while en route to the Maelstrom, and even they were only able to hold on for a few hours before being forced to conduct a fighting retreat and escape into the surrounding swamplands. Within thirty-six hours of Abaddon's arrival, Atika was claimed in the name of the Dark Gods.

THE BLOOD MARCH

The Catachan Jungle Fighters that had escaped the city were forced to battle their way through Pythos' predator-infested jungles, harried all the way by Black Legion murder squads. It is unlikely that any other Imperial Guard troops could have survived such a march, and even the Catachans suffered dreadfully through the ordeal. Battling their way past ambushes, fighting off attacks by massive reptilian monsters and voracious man-eating plants, the Catachans finally reached the relative safety of the Olympax mountain range, just 150 miles to the east of Atika.

Here, they braced themselves for an all-out attack by the Black Legion. Mysteriously, however, they were allowed time to regroup. Although the Black Legion continued to harry the Catachans, no serious attack on them was undertaken, and this gave the Imperial forces time to link up with each other.

Although the largest concentration of Imperial troops had been located at Atika, all of the delver-strongholds had their own garrisons and, in aggregate, these troops numbered in the tens of thousands. Colonel 'Death' Strike, commander of the 183rd regiment, and now de-facto Imperial Governor of Pythos, quickly began to organize these widely scattered forces, using commandeered sky barges to gather a sizable army at his base camp in the Olympax mountains. Within a fortnight, he began planning offensive operations against the Chaos invaders of what he now considered to be his planet.

Hidden beneath the surface of Pythos, the Damnation Cache was a portal to the Realm of Chaos itself.

THE DAMNATION CACHE

What Colonel Strike could not possibly know was that Abaddon had been far from idle. Unbeknownst to any of the Imperial citizens on the planet, Atika was built atop a hellish gateway known as the Damnation Cache. This gateway was a small but terrifyingly stable portal into the Warp, through which daemonic legions could travel into the material realm. Once it was captured, Abaddon would be able to summon forth a tide of wrathful Daemons to overwhelm the remaining defenders of Pythos and threaten the hundreds of Imperial planets nearby.

In the dark days of the Horus Heresy, vast numbers of Daemons had emerged from the Damnation Cache to fight against those who had remained loyal to the Emperor. Following Horus' defeat, the Damnation Cache was sealed, and in the centuries that followed, it disappeared from history. Only the Daemon-hunting Grey Knights retained any knowledge of the portal.

So it was that when Pythos was reclaimed as an Imperial colony in M33, none but the Grey Knights, the Chaos Gods, and the few surviving Chaos Space Marines that had fought there in the Heresy knew of the horrors hidden beneath the planet's surface. However, Abaddon was one of those Traitor Legion veterans, and immediately upon his arrival on Pythos, he began the task of breaking through the wards that had been set on that infernal gateway thousands of years before.

Disabling the wards was no easy task; dozens of Abaddon's most powerful sorcerers struggled to weaken the seals, sacrificing hundreds of Atika's citizens in bloody rituals of unbinding as they did so. One by one, the ancient bindings broke, until finally, just over a month after Abaddon's warfleet had first appeared in the system, the last ward was broken and the Damnation Cache was unsealed.

Immediately, the portal into the Warp reopened and a tide of Daemons gushed through, rampaging out of Atika, across the planet, and surging towards Colonel Strike's composite army. This time, the Catachans and their PDF allies were at least at combat readiness, but nothing could have prepared them for the tidal wave of destruction that the opening of the Damnation Cache had released.

A desperate struggle erupted on the lower slopes of Mount Olympax, as wave after wave of daemonic creatures crashed against the bastions and defence lines of Colonel Strike's camp. Only great heroics and terrible sacrifice prevented the base from being overrun in the first assault. Even so, it was clear to Colonel Strike that defending the newly established base camp could only result in the destruction of his entire command. Huddled together in a single location, they were an easy a target for the overwhelming hordes of Daemons pouring forth from the Damnation Cache.

COLONEL 'DEATH' STRIKE

Colonel Strike was the commander of the 183rd regiment of Catachan Jungle Fighters at the start of the Pandorax Incursion. He earned his nickname when still only a squad Sergeant, fighting against insurgents in the dense forests of Burlion VIII. His opponents said that fighting against Strike and his men meant only one thing – certain death. The 183rd regiment was en route to the Maelstrom war zone when catastrophic engine failure on their transport craft resulted in them being stranded on Pythos just before Abaddon's invasion began. Commander Azrael later said that were it not for Colonel Strike, Pythos would have been completely overrun.

183rd Catachan Jungle Fighters tattoos

183rd Catachan Jungle Fighters Regimental Banner

ADMIRAL KRANSWAR

Lord Admiral Orson Kranswar came from a renowned line of naval officers that had served the Emperor for millennia. He distinguished himself as a young midshipman, and was quickly promoted. Although personally brave, his tactics were predictable and lacked imagination – a trait exploited by his opponents during the space battles for the Adamantium Fields. He died leading a counter-attack when his flagship, the Revenge, *was boarded by Abaddon's Chaos Space Marines.*

Bitterly, Colonel Strike ordered the troops under his command to split up and retreat to the hundreds of delver-strongholds that were located all across Pythos. He knew that while no single settlement could resist attack, the sheer number of strongholds and their scattered locations offered the best chance of some Imperial forces surviving until reinforcements arrived. If, that was, reinforcements arrived at all…

BATTLEFLEET DEMETER

Although Abaddon's initial attack had been terrifyingly swift, he could not stop all messages calling for aid from being transmitted. High atop Atika, the desperate defenders had been able to hold out long enough for an astropathic distress signal to be sent streaking through the Immaterium. Despite the efforts of covens of Chaos Sorcerers aboard Abaddon's flagship, the Black Legion were unable to block all of these signals, which continued to be broadcast until bloodthirsty assault squads of Khorne Berserkers were finally able to smash their way into the astropathic chamber in Atika's central spire.

The Pandorax System lies a short distance to the galactic south of the Maelstrom, in the Demeter Sector. Lying so close to Huron Blackheart's realm meant that the Demeter Sector was in a high state of battle-readiness and could react to the attack quickly. Immediately upon receiving the distress call, the closest reserve fleet in the sector was ordered to the Pandorax System. Meanwhile, transport was arranged for the 19th and 27th Imperial Guard armies, as the massive resources of the Imperium swung into operation to repel Abaddon's invasion.

Battlefleet Demeter's reserve fleet was under the command of Lord Admiral Orson Kranswar, aboard his flagship, the *Revenge*. He was highly experienced, having fought numerous actions against Red Corsairs raiding fleets, though his background would offer little benefit against the overwhelming force of battle-scarred opposition he would encounter in the Pandorax System. Over the coming weeks and months, his fleet would fight in some of the largest space battles since the Gothic campaign.

The first omen of what Battlefleet Demeter would have to endure in the coming months occurred as soon as the fleet entered the Pandorax System. The 129th Imperial Destroyer Squadron was ranging ahead of the main fleet, and had just begun to pick its way through the asteroid belt that fringed the outer reaches of the star system. As they did so, they were subjected to a lightning-fast attack by Iconoclast destroyers hidden in the belt. Two Imperial ships were lost, and the Chaos squadron escaped unharmed, disappearing amidst the dense asteroid belt just minutes after launching their attack.

Kranswar first established a base on the tiny planet of Gaea, located on the edge of the Pandorax System. With his lines of communication secure, he then began to mount a series of raids and attacks into the asteroid field, intent on clearing a path to Pythos. In the following weeks, a series of increasingly brutal conflicts were fought in and around the asteroid belt, earning it the nickname of the 'Adamantium Fields' due to the myriad hulls of wrecked ships that floated there. At first, the ships of Abaddon's fleet held the upper hand, inflicting heavy losses on the Imperial flotillas as they repeatedly attempted to pick a way through the asteroid belt. However, in the long run, this was a campaign Abaddon could not hope to win, as the material superiority of his adversary – and the willingness of the Imperium to accept stunning losses to break through to Pythos – slowly but surely eroded the strength of the Chaos fleet.

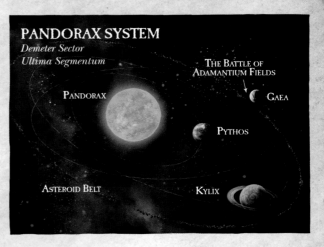

PANDORAX SYSTEM

Demeter Sector
Ultima Segmentum

PANDORAX

THE BATTLE OF ADAMANTIUM FIELDS

GAEA

PYTHOS

ASTEROID BELT

KYLIX

Slowly the tide began to turn, and Abaddon was forced to commit ever more ships to holding Kranswar in check. It was at this point that Abaddon received vital assistance in the form of a raiding fleet of Red Corsairs.

None can say if this came about because Abaddon and Huron Blackheart had agreed to aid each other, or simply because the Red Corsairs were drawn to the Pandorax System by the lure of conflict, just as the giant megaloshark of the Phythosian oceans is drawn to injured prey by the scent of blood in the water.

IMPERIAL BATTLE FLEET

Revenge, *Emperor class battleship*

Stalwart, *Dictator class cruiser*

Steel Anvil, *Dominator class cruiser*

Leviathan, *Lunar class cruiser*

Lord Solar, *Lunar class cruiser*

Courageous, *Dauntless class light cruiser*

Banshee, *Dauntless class light cruiser*

Myrmidon, *Endeavour class light cruiser*

Gamma Squadron, *three Sword class frigates*

Jaguar Squadron, *two Firestorm class frigates*

129th Destroyer Squadron, *six Cobra class destroyers*

89th Escort Squadron, *five Falchion class escorts*

In any case, the outcome was the same: combining their strength, the Chaos fleets swiftly drove the Imperial ships out of the Adamantium Fields, and back towards their base at Gaea. As they did so, the dispersed squadrons of ships belonging to the two sides gathered for a final space battle of such scale that it would be remembered for a hundred generations.

THE BATTLE FOR PANDORAX 960.M41

Lord-Admiral Kranswar knew that he was in a dangerous position. Although the number of escort vessels under his command roughly matched those in the combined Chaos fleets, he was heavily

> 'Our actions upon this day will determine if our names will live in glory or be despised. Launch all attack squadrons and prepare to engage the enemy! Let us win glory!!'
>
> – Admiral Kranswar, Battle for Pandorax

outgunned and outnumbered in terms of capital ships. The only real advantage he held lay in the number of fast attack craft he had; the launch bays on the *Revenge* and *Stalwart* gave him a two-to-one advantage over those carried by the Chaos ships.

In order to maximize this strength, Kranswar decided to hold the *Revenge* and *Stalwart* back, while the rest of his ships advanced to engage the Chaos fleet. While the bulk of his ships tried to keep the Chaos fleet at arm's length, his two carriers would launch successive waves of attack craft, tasked with overwhelming the squadrons defending the Chaos ships, and inflicting as much damage as possible. Hopefully, by the time the two fleets came to grips properly, the attack craft would have wreaked enough destruction to even the odds in the ensuing gun battle.

Unfortunately for Kranswar, while his plan was strategically sound, it lacked guile. Although Abaddon was still on Pythos commanding the ground campaign, his chosen lieutenant, Chaos Warlord Malgar Irongrasp, was a veteran of hundreds of space battles and had guessed what Kranswar's strategy was likely to be even before his sensors picked up the positions of the ships in the Imperial battlefleet.

1a & 1b. The Imperial advance flotilla engages Chaos fleet.

2. Chaos Space Marines and Daemons board the Revenge.

3. The Might of Huron *is destroyed by the* Stalwart *and the Dark Angels Battle Barge* Unrelenting Fury.

4. The Dark Angels fleet joins forces with the Imperial advance flotilla. The Chaos fleet is forced to retreat.

5a & 5b. The Chaos fleet is caught between the two Imperial forces, who inflict terrible damage to the Chaos ships before they can finally reach the safety of the Adamantium Fields. The Imperial victory is complete.

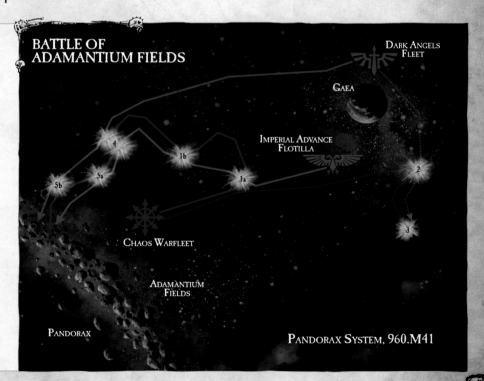

BATTLE OF ADAMANTIUM FIELDS

DARK ANGELS FLEET

GAEA

IMPERIAL ADVANCE FLOTILLA

CHAOS WARFLEET

ADAMANTIUM FIELDS

PANDORAX

PANDORAX SYSTEM, 960.M41

Irongrasp's ships tore forth from the Adamantium Fields like a battering ram, striking straight towards the heart of Kranswar's leading flotillas. Smashing through the screen of Imperial attack craft, they gave Kranswar's ships no time to carry out the dainty manoeuvres that he had transmitted to his command.

A furious close range battle erupted, as the Chaos fleet ploughed in amongst the ships of the Imperial advance guard, their immense, rippling broadsides illuminating their flanks. Hundreds of attack craft swirled and battled around the miles-long capital ships, while squadrons of escort vessels engaged in deadly close range gunnery battles.

Kranswar desperately ordered his ships to disengage. Although they had suffered heavy damage, they had given as good as they'd gotten, and if he could just buy enough time to rearm and refuel his now depleted attack craft, the battle could still be won. The Imperial ships executed Kranswar's orders with a stoicism bought through many long hours of careful training. The Imperial capital ships, screened by their escorts, broke away from the Chaos fleet, while the surviving attack craft headed back to the *Revenge* and *Stalwart* to re-arm.

However, Irongrasp had foreseen this reaction too. Unnoticed at the back of the Chaos warfleet, the *Might of Huron*, a Slaughter class cruiser, fired up the huge thruster arrays which define ships of that infamous class, and powered full speed ahead towards the Imperial carrier ships to the rear of the Imperial formation. Mysteriously, its tractors dragged a huge asteroid along behind it.

The purpose of the asteroid was revealed as the *Might of Huron* closed with the *Revenge* and *Stalwart*: the interior of the massive rock was hollow, and inside were hidden scores of Black Legion and Red Corsairs boarding parties, supported by Dreadclaw assault pods and short-ranged orbital flyers. As it neared the *Revenge*, the *Might of Huron* released the asteroid, which drifted directly towards the Imperial craft.

As soon as it was close enough, tractor beams inside the asteroid grappled the Imperial battleship, and chanting covens of Chaos Sorcerers loosed a barrage of

psychic attacks that tore down the Imperial ship's defensive shields and blinded its short-range batteries.

As soon as the *Revenge's* energy shields went down, hundreds of assault pods were launched at the now defenceless craft, and a massive boarding action erupted amidst the launch bays and corridors of the ship. The Chaos Space Marines in the boarding parties were quickly reinforced by hosts of horrifying Daemons, which poured from Warp portals that began appearing all across the ship. Within moments, the *Revenge* was engulfed in a furious battle.

Leaving the boarding parties to deal with the *Revenge*, the *Might of Huron* went after the *Stalwart*, which was ill-suited to a close-range gun battle with the heavily armed Chaos craft. At a stroke, Warlord Irongrasp had turned the tables on the Imperial fleet, negating any advantage the Imperial attack craft might have given them, and leaving them fatally split.

Meanwhile, the rest of the Chaos fleet was able to concentrate on crushing the ships of Kranswar's advance guard. Once these ships were destroyed, Irongrasp could finish off the *Revenge* and *Stalwart*, if anything remained after the brutal pummelling each was sustaining.

As Admiral Kranswar took personal command of one of the security battalions, he knew that his command was almost certainly doomed to destruction. He offered his soul to the immortal Emperor, for it would take a miracle to save his fleet.

CHAOS FLEET

Relentless Ire,
Desolator class battleship

Divine Corruption, *Repulsive class grand cruiser*

Heartless Destroyer, *Styx class heavy cruiser*

Helspite, *Carnage class cruiser*

Purgator Squadron, three *Idolator class raiders*

Savage Squadron, four *Iconoclast class destroyers*

Black Death Squadron, three *Iconoclast class destroyers*

RED CORSAIRS

Might of Huron, *Slaughter class cruiser*

Deathblade, *Murder class cruiser*

No Redemption, *Murder class cruiser*

Red Fury Squadron, three *Infidel class raiders*

Sanguine Slaughter Squadron, two *Iconoclast class destroyers*

MIGHT OF HURON
Slaughter class cruiser
Battle for Pandorax

COMMANDER AZRAEL

Commander Azrael is the present Supreme Grand Master of the Dark Angels Chapter. Azrael is a dynamic leader who knows and speaks his mind and is utterly convinced of the rightness of his cause. He fearlessly leads the Chapter in battle, commanding one of the mightiest, and most enigmatic, fighting forces in the galaxy. Azrael is also the guardian of the secrets the Dark Angels have locked away within the dark chambers hidden miles below the surface of The Rock, where only the Watchers in the Dark dare to tread.

A ROCK AND A HARD PLACE 960.M41

It was at this vital juncture that the navigators in both fleets began picking up signs of an opening in the Warp, indications that one or more ships were just about to jump into the system. The navigators could hardly believe their senses – appearing this close to a planetary body was almost suicidal. Nonetheless, the sensors didn't lie: where one moment there was nothing, in the next moment four capital ships and half a dozen escort craft blinked into existence.

Seconds later, an eleventh, impossibly vast, craft appeared; one that dwarfed even the asteroid Irongrasp had used to attack the *Revenge*. This mighty vessel was the Rock. At the moment of darkest despair, the Dark Angels had arrived.

As the Rock and its escorting craft moved to engage the main strength of the Chaos fleet, the Dark Angels Battle Barge *Unrelenting Fury* and three Hunter class escorts swept towards the stricken *Revenge*. Closing quickly, *Unrelenting Fury* launched a volley of boarding torpedoes towards

the Chaos asteroid. Just as they struck, a phalanx of Terminators teleported onto the rocky surface of the planetoid, their pale armour a beacon against the dark bulk – this was one of those rare times when the Deathwing deployed at their full strength, an event unlikely to occur more than once in a century.

They tore into the covens of Chaos Sorcerers on the asteroid with righteous fury, inflicting dozens of casualties even before the Chaos forces knew what had hit them. Moments later, the Dark Angels' boarding torpedoes struck, and with incredible swiftness, the asteroid was engulfed in a battle.

NOTABLE DARK ANGELS VESSELS
- *The Rock*
- Unrelenting Fury, *Battle Barge*
- Sword of Caliban, *Strike Cruiser*
- Fortitude Squadron, *three Hunter class destroyers*
- Terminatus Squadron, *three Hunter class destroyers*

Help was also at hand for the *Revenge*. A silvered Strike Cruiser arrived alongside the Dark Angels fleet, and a full brotherhood of Grey Knights materialized within the *Revenge's* hull to cut a swathe through the Daemon legions swarming through it. They were soon joined by contingents of Dark Angels, aiding the defenders and stemming the tide of the Chaos boarding parties' attacks.

LION'S CLAW SQUADRON

These Hunter class destroyers were the first Dark Angels ships to enter battle at the Adamantium Fields, and provided vital orbital support to Imperial ground forces throughout the reconquest of Pythos.

As the covens on the asteroid died, the portals through which the Daemons were appearing closed one by one. Hunting parties led by squads of Grey Knights wiped out the last of the Daemons lurking within the ship. Within hours, no taint of the incursion remained. Although she had been dreadfully damaged, the *Revenge* was saved, and would continue her vital role in the Pandorax campaign.

All around Gaea, the story was the same. The arrival of the Dark Angels swiftly turned the tide against Chaos. The first to feel the Dark Angels' avenging fury was the *Might of Huron*, which was blasted into oblivion by the combined firepower of the *Unrelenting Fury* and the attack squadrons launched from the *Stalwart*.

Meanwhile, Warlord Irongrasp found his ships trapped between the battered but still combat-worthy ships of Battlefleet Demeter, and the newly arrived Space Marine Strike Cruisers and escort squadrons. Surrounded on all sides, Irongrasp attempted to break through to the relative safety of the Adamantium Fields, but his fleet, already damaged in the earlier battles around Gaea, could not succeed. Only half of the ships in the Chaos fleet survived the battle, and those that did were so badly damaged that it would take years to repair them all.

Tragically, Admiral Kranswar was slain when he led a defence detail against the renegades that had invaded his flagship, and he did not live to see the fruits of his victory. The triumph of the Imperial forces in space was almost total, leaving Abaddon and his Black Legion trapped and cut off on the surface of Pythos.

THE RECONQUEST OF PYTHOS, 960.M41

If Abaddon was worried by this turn of events, he showed no sign. In the months since Pythos had been invaded, the planet had become a Daemon-infested hell. Greater Daemons revelled in battle against the saurian monsters that inhabited the planet, and hordes of lesser Daemons marched on the delver-strongholds.

Whenever this gibbering army reached one of the mountain fortresses, it launched a furious attack, aided by contingents of Black Legion warriors and Red Corsairs sent by Huron Blackheart to aid Abaddon's forces. Although the defenders of the strongholds put up a valiant resistance, they could not hope to hold out for very long. One by one, the strongholds were overrun, and any survivors were marched back to Atika as slaves.

KREATOR REX

Kreator Rex became one of the first members of the mysterious Chaos machine cult known as the Obliterators. He took part in all of the bloodiest battles of the Horus Heresy, building machines that combined the arts he had learnt with the twisting power of the Chaos. He now fights at Abaddon's side, building massive Chaos war engines to carry out the Despoiler's bidding. The Brass Scorpions, Towers of Skulls, Plaguereapers and Lords of Skulls he constructed proved vital in the attacks on Pythos' delver-strongholds during the Pandorax campaign, quickly breaching their walls and spear-heading every assault.

ORDER OF BATTLE:
THE PYTHOS INCURSION, 785960.M41

Pythos Planetary Defence Force
- *183rd Catachan Jungle Fighters regiment*
- *100 Delver-stronghold Militia battalions*

Pythos Reconquest Force
- *The Dark Angels Chapter*
- *One Brotherhood of Grey Knights*
- *4th, 15th, 22nd, and 99th Cadian regiments*
- *5th Mordian regiment*
- *One regiment Cadian Whiteshields*
- *116th Death Korps of Krieg regiment*
- *3rd, 8th Cadian Recon regiment*
- *10th Cadian Armoured regiment*
- *116th Vostroyan Armoured regiment*
- *1st, 5th Cadian Artillery regiments*
- *'Thunderers' Super-heavy Company*
- *Demeter 1st – 3rd Imperial Navy Fighter wings*
- *Demeter 1st – 2nd Imperial Navy Bomber wings*

Chaos Incursion Force
- *Abaddon's Black Legion: 26 warbands*
- *Kreator's Chaos War Engines: 7 Great Engines, 12 Lesser Engines*
- *Corpulax's Plague Zombie Horde: 100,000 Plague Zombies*
- *Vassal Warbands: Chaos Space Marine warbands owing service to Abaddon the Despoiler*

Hosts of the Damnation Cache
- *Graknor's Legion: 18 Cohorts of Khornate Daemons*
- *Plaguetoad's Host: 21 Cohorts of Nurgle's Daemons*
- *The Nefarious Brethren: 8 Cohorts of Tzeentchian Daemons*
- *Vangorian's Host: 9 Cohorts of Tzeentch Daemons*
- *Exstatix's Legion: 13 Cohorts of Slaaneshi Daemons*

PYTHOS RECONQUEST FORCE BATTLE STANDARDS

Army Standard, 27th Imperial Guard Army

Army Standard, 19th Imperial Guard Army

Army Standard, Pythos Reconquest Supreme Command
Pythos Planetary Defence Forces were subordinate to the Reconquest Supreme Command.

Army Badge, Pythos Reconquest Force
A number of ad-hoc variations of this badge were used by military units during the campaign, and it was not universally used by all formations taking part in the campaign.

What the slaves returned to was not the city they once knew. Located so close to the corrupting force of the Damnation Cache, Atika had changed beyond all recognition. Strange, hideously mutated structures had sprouted from the once elegant spire walls. Most of the city had been abandoned, and the population now lived in the network of twisted underground tunnels and caverns that surrounded the Damnation Cache. Vile smoke and putrid vapours filled the air in the tunnels and belched out through cracks and crevices into the surrounding atmosphere. Most terrible of all, the enslaved population of the city had been struck down by a terrible plague that reduced them to shambling creatures, more dead than alive.

It was this grim scene of devastation and despair that greeted the victors of the space battles in the Adamantium Fields. Finally arriving in orbit above the planet, the Imperial fleet immediately began orbital bombardments on the daemonic armies that were assaulting the delver-strongholds. Squadrons of Marauder Bombers intensified the bombardment, aided by Xerxes Airborne Support Wings, and Dark Angels Thunderhead and Talon of Vengeance squadrons.

Abaddon's forces were driven back by the overwhelming aerial barrages, allowing companies of Space Marines and regiments of Imperial Guard to relieve the defenders, many of whom had been fighting continuously for over a year. In a brief ceremony, Colonel Strike officially handed over command of the planetary defence force to Commander Azrael. Colonel Strike refused all offers to join the other high commanders in the orbiting battlefleet, preferring to return to the fray in his specially modified Baneblade *Traitor's Bane*, so that he could fight against the invaders who had cost him so many men.

However, although the tide was turning, the Chaos armies continued their relentless assaults on the delver-strongholds. No sooner was one strike driven off, than a new one would begin. Abaddon's tactics changed; instead of making overwhelming and methodical attacks against the strongholds closest to Atika, his legions, supplemented by Hounds of Huron raiding parties, attacked wherever the defenders were weakest.

No matter how well Azrael organised his forces to react to these attacks, he could not always arrive in time. Many smaller strongholds were overrun and their populations enslaved. It quickly became clear to Azrael that fire-fighting in this way was leading nowhere. He had to strike at the source of the problem: the Damnation Cache itself would need to be recaptured and resealed.

In truth, the Grey Knights accompanying the Dark Angels had been arguing for just such a strike ever since the fleet had arrived over the beleaguered world. Although the Dark Angels harbour a bitter hatred for Abaddon and his allies, Azrael argued that the first priority of the Emperor's armies on Pythos was to shield and protect the planet's citizens; therefore, the delver-strongholds should be saved before Atika was attacked. It was only when it became clear that Abaddon's forces would continue to launch sporadic attacks against the strongholds, no matter how well protected they were, that Azrael was forced to change his tactics.

ASSAULT ON ATIKA, 961.M41

Once the decision was made, the Imperial forces acted quickly to bring the Emperor's wrath to their daemonic foes. The assault on Atika was announced by a massive orbital bombardment. The once-gleaming spire-city toppled to the ground, and the surrounding area was pounded into wasteland by the combined firepower of the Imperial fleet. In the wake of the bombardment, Thunderhawk Gunships and Drop Pods crashed onto the ravaged battlefield, disgorging the full strength of the Dark Angels Chapter, supported by the

Grey Knights who had saved the *Revenge*. Even the Black Legion and the hordes of Daemons at Abaddon's command could not resist such a hammer blow, and they were quickly driven underground by the fury of the Imperial attack.

The second wave of the assault swiftly followed. Scores of orbital transporters landed around the bridgehead the Space Marines had established, disgorging regiment after regiment of Imperial Guard onto the steaming mire left by the orbital attack. Colonel Strike was one of the first to land amidst the ruins of the city; the hoary survivor had been given command of the Imperial Guard assault army by Azrael himself, and was determined to see the campaign to its brutal conclusion.

The Imperial Guard regiments arrived not a moment too soon, as wave after wave of vile Daemons poured forth from the ravaged underground tunnels, having scented blood. Many Imperial Guard platoons and their accompanying armoured support had only just mustered in their positions at the perimeter of the bridgehead when the daemonic horde struck. Lasguns and battle-cannon tore gaping holes in the charging ranks of Daemons, but as one infernal creature fell, ten more stood ready to take its place.

Soon the whole Imperial frontline was engulfed in a terrible melee, as Guardsmen and Space Marines battled furiously against creatures spawned by the Warp. Bayonets were fixed and chainswords activated in a desperate defence against the talons and blades of the daemonic host. Then, the guns of the orbiting Imperial fleet fired into the Warp-spawned horde, the massive macro cannon shells and strikes of their lance batteries smashing into the ground dangerously close to the hand-to-hand combats being fought all around the bridgehead. Each titanic blast lifted scores of bodies into the air to fall amongst the swirling combatants.

Even the warp-spawned Daemon horde could not withstand such hammer blows, and against the massed firepower of the fleet, the attack faltered and finally stopped. Around the implacable Space Marines, the weary, wounded guardsmen drew breath, relieved to see tunnel mouths empty and quiet. All around the bridgehead, the ground was covered in

2nd Company Vehicle Pennant, 1st Cadian Artillery Regiment

The Mk19c Jungle Pattern camouflage scheme was adopted by the 1st Cadian Artillery Regiment at Pandorax.

Kreator Rex marks all of the war engines he creates with his personal rune of forging.

Battle Standard borne by Graknor's Legion.

CORPULAX, THE PLAGUE LORD

Corpulax is a Plague Marine and Chaos Warlord. He was originally a member of the Consecrators Chapter, but was infected with the Zombie Plague when battling against the foetid forces of Typhus. Left for dead on a devastated planet, Corpulax awoke as a reanimated corpse. However, unlike so many of the plague's victims, Corpulax retained his intelligence and cognitive powers. Over the last three hundred years, he has orchestrated an inexorable rise to power, finally becoming one of Abaddon's most trusted warlords. He has fought in dozens of battles, either at Abaddon's side or carrying out his bidding. Wherever he appears, he spreads the terrible plague with which he is afflicted, and is single-handedly responsible for disseminating the disease that wiped out every inhabitant of the city of Atika.

the slowly dematerialising remains of more than 100,000 Daemons. Within an hour, the bodies were gone, returned to the Realm of Chaos that had spawned them. They left the battlefield eerily barren, strewn only with Imperial corpses and the blackened shells of wrecked tanks.

THE UNDERGROUND WAR

With the bridgehead established, Azrael began the grim task of clearing a path to the Damnation Cache itself. The underground tunnels and caverns were defended bitterly by newly summoned Daemons and Chaos Space Marines under Abaddon's command, but the Imperial attackers were implacable.

The cave system was vast, and incredibly complex. Tunnels branched and intertwined, some of them narrowing so that even infantry could only advance in single file, while others were so massive that they formed vast underground caverns large enough to allow Deathstrike Vortex Missile batteries and hunting packs of Warhound Titans to bring their long-range weapons to bear. Unnumbered battles and firefights were fought within the Stygian darkness below Atika, but slowly, yard by yard, the Imperial forces battled their way through the darkened tunnels.

As they closed in upon the Damnation Cache, the Daemons and Chaos Space Marines were joined by shambling hordes of mutant zombies. These were the surviving remnants of the once-

proud citizens of Atika, enslaved ever since Abaddon had captured the planet, and now horrifically transformed by the warping effects of the Chaos portal. Gritting their teeth, the Imperial attackers forged on through their foes, every step taking them closer to the Damnation Cache itself.

Even though the situation around the cache was becoming increasingly desperate, Abaddon continued to launch raids on the delver-strongholds, even leading several of the attacks personally. Azrael, however, no longer allow this to distract him from his purpose. Spearheaded by the Dark Angels and Grey Knights, the forces of Chaos were driven ever further back until the Damnation Cache was almost in Imperial hands.

However, just as Abaddon seemed defeated, a fresh flotilla of Red Corsairs raiders suddenly appeared in the system. Breaking through the Imperial cordon, they rendezvoused with Abaddon in the jungle, and their orbital transport craft quickly evacuated the surviving Chaos Space Marines from locations scattered all over Pythos. Although the Imperial fleet was able to destroy some of the Red Corsairs' transporters, the majority made it to the ships hidden in orbit, and escaped. Hours later, an Imperial assault seized the Damnation Cache, and the Grey Knights began the arduous process of re-establishing the wards that would seal it once again. The Pandorax Incursion had finally been defeated, but at huge cost.

Valkyrie, 1st Squadron, 3rd Cadian Recon regiment

Valkyrie, 5th Squadron, 3rd Cadian Recon regiment

PYTHOSIAN CRYSTAL

Pythos' main exports are high-quality ruby crystals, found in abundance in the cave systems that honeycomb the planet's mountains. The crystals are a vital component in many types of Imperial laser weaponry. Gathering the crystals is fraught with peril, as the caves are also home to a frightening array of deadly creatures, many of which are semi-intelligent and perfectly willing to hunt down the delvers that enter their territories. Barges transport the crystals from the strongholds to Atika, where they are transported off-planet.

AFTERMATH, 961.M41 - PRESENT

In the wake of Abaddon's escape and the resealing of the Damnation Cache, the Dark Angels and Grey Knights left Pythos. Colonel Strike was left in command of the two Imperial Guard armies that had taken part in the reconquest, and has been fighting a decades-long campaign to cleanse the planet of any lingering daemonic infestation ever since. Although the Damnation Cache was resealed, the damage it inflicted was severe, and many minor Warp rifts still need to be closed. The war carries on to this day.

Why Abaddon attacked the Pandorax System remains a mystery. However, there are recurring rumours that his aim was not one of conquest, but of discovery. It is said that the Ruinous Powers sent Abaddon a vision which revealed that, hidden among the population of Pythos, he would find a powerful psyker whose latent abilities would ensure victory in his coming crusade against the Imperium.

Decades later, the Dark Angels heard whispers that a mysterious psyker of prodigious power had ordered the capture of an artefact known only as the Hellfire Stone. These rumours were confirmed when a Dark Angels force clashed with Chaos renegades searching for the artefact on the Imperial planet known as Bane's Landing. In his sanctum, Azrael remembered the campaign he had fought against Abaddon all those years before. Perhaps, he thought as he made the connection, Abaddon was not defeated on Pythos at all. Perhaps he had left because he had acquired exactly what he had been looking for…

DARK PINION

Deathlord Blackfire's Heldrake, Dark Pinion, destroyed more Imperial aircraft than any other flyer in the campaign. Left behind when Abaddon retreated, he harries Imperial forces to this day from a secret lair in the Hollowfal mountains.

THE PANDORAX INCURSION TIMELINE

The Pandorax Incursion took place between 959.M41 and 960.M41, when a Chaos Space Marine warfleet under the command of the infamous Abaddon the Despoiler invaded the Pandorax system, in Imperial space.

M31: The Damnation Cache opens on the planet of Pythos during the Horus Heresy. It is a huge underground chamber within which Daemons can freely enter the mortal plane. Following Horus' defeat, the portal is sealed. It is forgotten by the Imperium in the millennia that follow.

M34: Imperial colonists settle Pythos and begin the difficult operation of mining precious minerals from the planet's mountain ranges.

959.M41: A Black Legion incursion fleet appears in orbit over Pythos and launches a planetary assault.

830959.M41: The Chaos Space Marines make an overwhelming attack, capturing Pythos' single major city, Atika.

833959.M41: Colonel Strike leads the remnants of his regiment of Catachan Jungle Fighters out of Atika on the Blood March. A week later the survivors reach the nearest delver-stronghold.

887959.M41: Imperial forces consolidate and start fighting back, led by Strike's rugged survivors.

899959.M41: The Battle For Khan's Stronghold. Delver militia hold out desperately against a Chaos Space Marine attack. Catachan Jungle Fighters commanded by Strike arrive just in time to save the stronghold, and inflict the first important defeat on Abaddon's forces since the incursion began.

913959.M41: The Black Legion unseal the Damnation Cache. Bitter conflict ensues, as the resultant horde of Daemons scatters the gathered Imperial defenders, and the Chaos Space Marines start to capture the planet's delver-strongholds one by one.

933959.M41: A swarm of Daemons appear suddenly and overrun Khan's Stronghold. The entire delver population is massacred and the stronghold is razed to the ground.

960.M41: Battlefleet Demeter sets out to relieve Pythos, bearing Imperial Guard infantry and armoured support.

519960.M41: Battlefleet Demeter arrives in Pandorax. A base is established on Gaea – an isolated planet on the edge of the system. The Imperial fleet is harried by constant attacks from Black Legion craft, but gradually begins to get the upper hand.

555960.M41: 1st Battle of Sunward Gap. As Imperial forces try to force a passage through the Admantium Fields, major engagements are fought to control the relatively clear path through the asteroid field known as Sunward Gap.

601960.M41: 2nd Battle of Sunward Gap.

649960.M41: The Imperial 120th Destroyer Squadron and Chaos Razorsnarl Squadron engage in a furious battle. The last surviving craft in the Chaos squadron self-destructs rather than be defeated, and the resulting explosion destroys the last ships in the Imperial Squadron, leaving no survivors from either side.

666960.M41: 3rd Battle of Sunward Gap.

755960.M41: A contingent of Red Corsairs ships arrive in the system, turning the tables on Battlefleet Demeter.

759960.M41: 4th Battle of Sunward Gap. The Imperial battlefleet is driven back by the reinforced Chaos fleet.

766960.M41: A major battle takes place around the Imperial base at Gaea. At the height of the battle, an Adeptus Astartes fleet led by the Rock dramatically arrives in-system. The Chaos fleet is crushed, and surviving ships are scattered and driven off. The way to Pythos lies open.

785960.M41: Imperial forces arrive over Pythos. The planet is now infested with Daemons, and many of the delver-strongholds have been captured. A terrible plague has broken out in Atika, turning Imperial prisoners into mindless zombie slaves. Several major battles are fought as Imperial forces start to cleanse the planet of Daemons, but the Black Legion's attacks on the remaining strongholds are relentless.

799960.M41: In an unholy alliance, four Greater Daemons belonging to each of the Chaos powers materialize inside the walls of the major delver-stronghold known as High Peak. The four rampage through the lightly-protected stronghold, killing almost nine tenths of the population before vanishing back to the Realm of Chaos.

847960.M41: Contact is mysteriously lost with the three delver-strongholds located on Glazer's Plateau. Dark Angels Scouts find that the populations of all three strongholds have been turned into plague zombies overnight. Azrael is left with no choice but to cleanse the zombie-infested plateau with a massive bombardment delivered by the Imperial fleet.

968960.M41: The Grey Knights finally convince Commander Azrael that the Damnation Cache must be captured and resealed.

085961.M41: A major orbital invasion is undertaken to re-capture Atika and the Damnation Cache. The initial landings are successful, but then the zombie hordes are unleashed and almost overrun the Imperial bridgehead. The zombies are only stopped by the massed firepower of the orbiting Imperial fleet.

099961.M41: Imperial forces clear a path from the landing sight to the entrances of the tunnels that lead to the Damnation Cache. Despite suffering heavy casualties, the combined Imperial army drives back Abaddon's forces, and secures the tunnel entrances.

102961.M41: Imperial attack teams start clearing the tunnels which access the Damnation Cache. The Daemons and Black Legion defend the tunnels furiously but the Imperials, led by the Dark Angels and Grey Knights, are implacable.

129961.M41: Mount Blizzard, the second largest delver-stronghold on Pythos, is almost completely overrun by a surprise attack from Chaos Space Marine forces led by both Abaddon and Khârn the Betrayer.

153961.M41: The Battle of Emerald Cave. Imperial forces fight the largest battle of the underground war in a huge cavern known as Emerald Cave. The cavern is so vast that both sides are able to employ aircraft and super-heavy war machines in a massive engagement lasting several days. It is only the direct intervention of Commander Azrael that secures an Imperial triumph.

188961.M41: Victory is within the Imperium's grasp when the Black Legion suddenly retreats, breaking through the line with support from a surprise attack by the Red Corsairs' naval forces.

190961.M41: The remaining daemonic forces in the cave network are swept aside by a final Imperial assault, and the Damnation Cache is finally recaptured and resealed.

961.M41 to present: After the Dark Angels and Grey Knights leave Pythos to deal with more pressing matters, Imperial Guard forces are left to cleanse the planet of Daemons. Although the Damnation Cache has been neutralised, the damage inflicted is severe, and there are many minor Warp rifts that still need to be closed. The war carries on to this day.

999.M41: The circumstances of the war fought to defeat the Traitor Marines in the Pandorax system were recorded in the Dark Angels' archives on their return to the Rock. These reports are unearthed and brought before the masters of the Chapter's Inner Circle again, decades later, during the Dark Vengeance campaign…

RESCUE THE REVENGE, 960.M41

The Imperial battleship *Revenge* has been overrun by Chaos Space Marines boarding parties and Chaos Daemons. Rushing to their aid is the Dark Angels Battle Barge *Unrelenting Fury* – but have they arrived in time to save the stricken battleship?

Outwitted by the admiral of the Chaos fleet, the Imperial flagship *Revenge* quickly became isolated and found itself under assault from Black Legion and Red Corsairs boarding parties hidden within a large asteroid, which had been pulled into position near the *Revenge* by a Chaos battle cruiser. The *Revenge*'s shields and protective batteries were disabled by a barrage of powerful psychic attacks, allowing boarding parties mounted in Dreadclaw assault pods to attack the ship from close quarters. Once on board, Chaos Sorcerers were able to open portals to the Warp, summoning waves of Daemons to aid them in overrunning the Imperial ship.

A furious battle erupted on the exposed flight decks of the *Revenge*. Her crew sprang into action, fighting desperately to repel the Chaos Space Marines and Daemons that now swarmed through their beloved ship. Lord-Admiral Kranswar ordered the Imperial Guard troops being transported in the *Revenge* to help clear the flight decks, before taking up arms himself and leading a squad of naval combat troops against the invaders. Meanwhile, just outside the ship, squadrons of short-range Imperial flyers attempted to battle their way to the Chaos asteroid, in a bid to kill – or at least distract – the covens of Chaos Sorcerers that were doing so much damage to the *Revenge*. The Imperial fighters and bombers were engaged by great flights of Chaos Space Marine Heldrakes launched from hidden chambers within the asteroid, and a swirling zero-g dogfight began in the airless void that lay between the asteroid and the *Revenge*.

On the Imperial ship, the forces of Chaos were starting to get the upper hand. Hordes of Daemons rampaged along its corridors and across the blood-spattered flight decks.

REVENGE
Emperor class battleship
Admiral Kranswar's flagship, Battlefleet Demeter

In a desperate bid to stem the tide, Admiral Kranswar ordered the Imperial Guard to use its armoured vehicles within the confines of the ship. Leman Russ battle tanks rumbled along any corridors that were wide enough to allow their passage, and massive transport lifts carried Baneblades and Shadowswords up to the larger flight decks. It was a futile gesture: the Imperial Guard vehicles could not make effective use of their long range weapons within the narrow confines of the ship, and were quickly surrounded and overrun. Before long, the ship was littered with the remnants of tanks from which the Daemons had torn the hatches and swept inside to butcher the unfortunate crews trapped within.

Kranswar did his best to rectify the dreadful situation. The *Revenge* was completely isolated, and what remained of his battlefleet could not come to his aid – indeed, it looked likely that the entire fleet was facing a swift, vicious destruction. Determining that his position was hopeless, the fatalistic Kranswar ordered his personal guards to accompany him as they battled their way through to the nearest of the *Revenge*'s main drives. If he could reach the engine room, he could set the ship's engines to overload. This would lead to the ultimate destruction of the *Revenge*, but would at least ensure she would not fall into Abaddon's hands. The naval ratings snapped to attention and prepared to carry out their Admiral's bidding without hesitation. They knew that death was nothing compared to the dishonour the Imperial fleet would suffer if the *Revenge* was captured.

It was at this moment of despair and doomed valour that help arrived. Unbeknownst to the Lord-Admiral, the Grey Knights had learned of Abaddon's presence, and more specifically of his re-opening of the Damnation Cache, sealed millennia before. The Grey Knights did not have the strength to halt Abaddon on their own and had been forced to approach the Dark Angels for aid. How exactly the Grey Knights were able to convince Supreme Grand Master Azrael to give them the help they needed is not known, but aid them he did, ordering his entire Chapter to the Pandorax System in order to foil Abaddon's scheme.

In responding to the Grey Knights' urgent request for aid, the Dark Angels arrived in the Pandorax System at the height of the battle for the *Revenge*. The Dark Angels' Battle Barge *Unrelenting Fury* swooped towards the stricken Imperial battleship. Once within range, the Deathwing were dispatched to the Chaos asteroid, and the brotherhood of Grey Knights accompanying them were teleported to the heart of the fighting within the *Revenge* itself. Thunderhawk Gunships and Drop Pods followed in their wake, and the fate of the *Revenge* hung in the balance…

THE HORDES OF CHAOS

Victory lies within the grasp of the Chaos army. One last push is all they need to overrun the Imperial flagship!

A cunning ruse by the Warlord of the Chaos fleet has opened the way for Chaos forces to board the Imperial flagship. However, with the *Revenge* almost overrun, the cursed followers of the false Emperor are starting to turn the tables. Ships belonging to the Dark Angels, one of the most intractable foes the servants of the Chaos gods have ever faced, have appeared nearby, and are rushing to save the *Revenge* from the Chaos boarding parties. This counter-attack must be stopped in its tracks, but without jeopardising the continuing battle against the Imperial forces trying to defend the ship. This will require that the attackers split their strength, allocating just enough troops to each task to ensure its success.

In addition to attacking the hated foe on these fronts, care must be taken to protect the covens of Chaos Sorcerers that breached the *Revenge's* defensive screens and are maintaining the portals to the Warp from their asteroid temple. Victory is assured if the Sorcerers can be protected from the vengeful Space Marines who have been sent to destroy them.

CHAOS ORDER OF BATTLE
The forces used in the Chaos army are listed below.

Traitor Boarding Force
- Maelstrom of Gore
- Legionnaire Warband
- Daemon Engine Pack

Asteroid Defence Force
- Thousand Sons War Coven
- Helbrute
- Chaos Terminator squad
- Possessed squad
- Khorne Berzerkers squad
- Raptors squad
- Warp Talons squad
- Thousand Sons squad
- 3 Chaos Space Marine squads
- 4 Defilers

Chaos Flyers
- 2 Heldrake Fear Squadrons

Asteroid Reserves Force
- Cult of Destruction
- Legionnaire Warband
- 2 Lords of Skulls
- Maulerfiend
- Forgefiend

Khorne's Daemon Horde
- Bloodthirster
- 2 Daemon Princes of Khorne
- Daemonic Forgehost
- Cohort of Blood

Tzeentch's Daemon Horde
- Lord of Change
- Flaming Host of Tzeentch

Nurgle's Daemon Horde
- Great Unclean One
- The Tallymen of Nurgle

Slaanesh's Daemon Horde
- Keeper of Secrets
- Herald of Slaanesh
- The Great Promenade of Exquisite Excess

CHAOS DEPLOYMENT
The Asteroid Defence Force deploys on the surface of any of the asteroids outside the *Revenge*, and the Traitor Boarding Force deploys in the Chaos deployment zone on the *Revenge*. One unit of up to ten models and one attached character must deploy in the Chaos deployment zone in the Defence Battery Control Room. Finally, the Chaos Flyers deploy in Deep Space within 12" of any asteroid. None of these units start in Strategic Reserve.

The remaining forces start in Strategic Reserve. The Asteroid Reserves Force must enter from the Chaos board edge (see map) or by moving onto the board through the Warp Portal, treating it as a friendly board edge. The Daemon Hordes do not use the Strategic Reserve table: instead, at the start of each Chaos turn, the Chaos players must pick one god's Daemon Horde. This horde must arrive that turn, either by Deep Striking or by moving onto the board through the Warp Portal, treating it as a friendly board edge. Any units from the chosen god's Daemon Horde that do not enter play on the nominated turn are lost.

CHAOS STRATEGIC ASSETS
The following Strategic Assets must be used by the Chaos army: **Death to the False Emperor!, Time of Vengeance, Blood Thirst, Grand Pavane, Lies of Tzeentch, Plaguestorm.**

CHAOS BATTLE PLAN
The Chaos players knew that they must take maximum advantage of their first turn superiority. To this end, they called on Khorne's Daemons first, as they were the most effective assault force. The boarding force would spearhead the first attack, stepping aside as the waves of Daemons arrived. They would fight a defensive battle on the asteroid, holding the Temple of Skulls and keeping the arriving Dark Angels from the *Revenge*.

REPEL BOARDERS

The Chaos assault is unstoppable at first, but the arrival of the Grey Knights and Dark Angels turns the tide.

At first it proved impossible for the Imperial Guard forces on board the *Revenge* to contain the Chaos boarding parties. Black Legion warbands and packs of Khorne Daemons tore into the Guardsmen, swamping them in a tide of gore. A Khorne Lord of Skulls rippled into existence through the Warp portal, adding its punishing fire to that of the Chaos Space Marines. It looked as if nothing could stop the forces of Chaos from overrunning the ship. Imperial Guard reserves were hurled onto the fray, quickly joined by the first Grey Knight Terminator squads to teleport onto the ship. The battle hung in the balance, as both sides fought to gain the upper hand.

Meanwhile, outside the ship, the superior numbers of Imperial Flyers managed to slowly but surely establish control of the space lanes, and were able to provide support for the Dark Angels as they attacked the Chaos Sorcerers on the asteroid. Deprived of support from outside, the Chaos boarding parties could not maintain the momentum of their attack, which started to falter, and then be driven back. The Imperium had secured a victory by the very narrowest of margins.

The battle for the Revenge *was but a precursor to the carnage that was to unfold upon Pythos. Bidding his battle-brothers leave the war-blasted* Revenge *and reconvene upon the surface of the planet, Grand Master Azrael prepared for the next phase of the war effort.*

Though the Chaos Space Marines had been forced to withdraw from the Revenge, *Abaddon swore that the ground war would be bloodier still.*

Grand Master Sammael led the Ravenwing against the Chaos Sorcerers on the asteroid in defence of the Revenge, and was at the forefront of many lightning assaults on the surface of Pythos.

Khârn the Betrayer led the main assault inside the Revenge itself.

Anathrax Blackmace boarded the Revenge in his Dreadclaw, cutting straight into the control room.

Admiral Kranswar made a heroic last stand in the belly of his flagship.

A cabal of Chaos Sorcerers kept the Warp rift open wide, allowing tides of Daemons to spill through.

Belial led the Deathwing's mass teleport onto the Chaos asteroid base.

Draigo, of the Grey Knights, slew a Daemon Prince atop the comms tower.

Garaagh'rkalla, Herald of Khorne, called upon the Blood God to blind the Grey Knights around him with insatiable bloodlust.

The Dark Angels Chapter was instrumental in the reconquest of the Pandorax system, from their arrival until the sealing of the Damnation Cache.

Deathwing Terminators teleported exactly where needed, striking across Pythos' surface.

Deathwing Knights fear no foe.

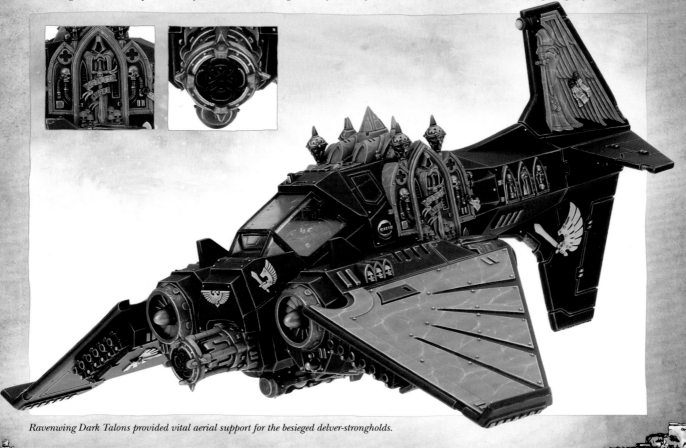

Ravenwing Dark Talons provided vital aerial support for the besieged delver-strongholds.

Interceptor Squads were used to counter Chaos surprise attacks.

Grey Knight with Warding Stave

Castellan Crowe

Ratling Snipers proved especially deadly in the cave-fighting beneath Atika.

Imperial Guard Sanctioned Pysker

Ogryn with ripper gun

Camouflaged Scout Sentinels stalked the jungles of Pythos.

Several Cadian regiments took part in the Pandorax campaign, earning great honour.

Veteran Catachan Jungle Fighters

Bloodletters from Graknor's Legion

Pink Horrors of Tzeentch belonging to The Nefarious Brethren

An Icon Bearer and Champion from Plaguetoad's Host

Daemonette Icon Bearer   A Seeker of Slaanesh from Exstatix's Legion

Black Legion Chaos Terminators caused annihilation wherever they were met.

Raptors attacked the defenders of the delver-strongholds from above.

The Black Legion fought throughout the campaign.

Khorne Berzerkers from Khârn the Betrayer's warband

The Khorne Lord of Skulls 'Crushing Death' wreaked bloody havoc within the Revenge's *hangar deck and was later involved in the last defence of the Damnation Cache itself upon Pythos.*

PANDORAX
RULES OF ENGAGEMENT

The Pandorax campaign included some of the largest and most bitter battles fought by Imperial forces in the last 100 years. Any of these battles will make an excellent subject for a game of Apocalypse.

On the following pages we have included additional Environmental Rules, Apocalypse Missions, Strategic Assets and Finest Hours, and Apocalypse Formations.

The missions and environmental rules presented here have been designed to represent the various environs of Pythos, as well as the unique battles the combatants engaged in during the campaign.

The Assets and Finest Hours allow you to recreate the strategies and heroics of Pandorax's champions and villains.

The additional Apocalypse Formations presented in this War Zone portray legendary units that fought in the war for the Pandorax System. Many of these units have fought a bitter, continual war since the time of the Horus Heresy, so they may be used in any Apocalypse game.

FORGING A NARRATIVE

The planet of Pythos is a death world; just one of many planets scattered across the Imperium that are inhabited by deadly local flora and fauna. If that wasn't bad enough, hidden beneath the surface of Pythos is a portal to the Warp. You should feel free to use the death world themed rules in this War Zone for battles set on other such planets, and the Daemon-themed rules to represent other incursions by the forces of Chaos. In addition, the rules for the battle for the spaceship *Revenge* can be used in space battles you fight.

WAR ZONE: PANDORAX TERRAIN

PYTHOS FLORA AND FAUNA

Pythos, the focus of the Pandorax campaign, is a death world home to a plethora of deadly flora and fauna. Some of the more commonly encountered creatures and types of unique terrain found on Pythos are described below.

DEATH WORLD JUNGLES

The jungle covering much of Pythos is a truly deadly environment. Most of the plants are toxic, and just brushing against them can be fatal. Other plants spew forth spores that can suffocate a man in a heartbeat if they are inhaled. Even worse are the swarms of insects flitting between the trees. Most of them have deadly stings and bites; however, the most horrific are those that lay their eggs in the living, which hatch into larva and consume the host from within.

Death world jungles are mysterious terrain. Roll on the following table to determine what rules apply to it.

DEATH WORLD JUNGLE MYSTERIOUS TERRAIN TABLE

2D6	JUNGLE TYPE
2-5	**Just Plain Dangerous:** The jungle is dangerous terrain. Catachan Jungle Fighters treat it as difficult terrain instead.
6-8	**Carnivorous Jungle:** See the Mysterious Forest terrain table in the *Warhammer 40,000* rulebook.
9	**Pythosian Pit-trap Glade:** See below.
10	**Deathglades:** See below.
11	**Pythosian Land Dragon Lair:** See page 36.
12	**Gargantor Herd:** See page 36.

PYTHOSIAN PIT-TRAP GLADE

Pythosian pit-trap plants appear at first glance to be relatively harmless patches of lesser spike-wart, but each conceals a trapdoor, beneath which lurks the semi-sentient pit-trap plant. Tendrils sense when a living creature approaches within a few feet of the trap, at which point the trapdoor flies open and up to a dozen thick vines spring out, enveloping the victim, and dragging them into the pit-trap. Under the ground lies a small pit filled with deadly digestive acid; they prey is first crushed to death, and then dropped into the pool of digestive juices to be consumed.

Any Infantry model within the glade at the start of their Shooting phase must pass a Strength test. If the test is failed, the victim is destroyed with no saving throws of any kind allowed.

DEATHGLADES

Many areas of Pythos are covered by its notorious deathglades. What makes the deathglades so dangerous are the numerous pools of bubbling, caustic liquid that dot their surface. These pools are fed by corrosive minerals that leak from the planet's core through vents in the bedrock. Anything that enters such a pool is almost instantly dissolved by the virulent acid, dying an agonizing death in seconds. Pythos' capital city, Atika, is located on the edge of a vast area of deathglades, an area of deadly swampland so inhospitable that few living creatures will venture into it. This offers a measure of protection for Atika, shielding the city from the massive predators inhabiting the jungles beyond the deathglades.

One randomly determined model in the unit that triggered the mysterious terrain roll is destroyed, with no saving throws of any kind allowed, and all other models treat the terrain feature as lethal terrain.

PYTHOSIAN LAND DRAGON LAIR

Land dragons are huge saurian predators, and the main reason Pythos is designated a death world. They are aggressive hunters, and will stalk anything that moves. Their main prey are gargantors, but a land dragon is more than happy to consume man-sized creatures. The land dragon's thick hide makes it very difficult to harm, while its dense, razor-sharp fangs are perfectly capable of biting through all but the thickest armour.

One randomly determined model in the unit that triggered the roll on the Mysterious Terrain table and all Infantry models within 3" of the terrain feature are destroyed, with no saving throws of any kind allowed. The terrain feature is lethal terrain until the land dragon is eliminated. In addition, any Infantry model which ends a move within 3" of the terrain feature is destroyed, with no saving throws of any kind allowed. In order to eliminate the land dragon, a unit must make a shooting attack, treating the terrain feature as the target. Roll To Hit as normal. The land dragon is eliminated if at least one weapon with a Strength of 8 or more scores a hit.

GARGANTOR HERD

The gargantor is a massive creature that feasts on the jungle's plants and trees. Although a herbivore, the gargantor has a vicious temperament. The charge of a herd of gargantors is almost unstoppable – each creature becomes a living battering ram, and is perfectly capable of flipping over a Leman Russ battle tank.

One randomly determined model in the unit that triggered the roll on the mysterious terrain table is immediately destroyed, with no saving throws of any kind allowed. Then make two rolls on the following table, one for the unit that triggered the roll, and one for the unit nearest to them (friend or foe). The herd then stampedes off the table and has no further effect on play.

GARGANTOR STAMPEDE TABLE

D6	UNIT IS NOT A VEHICLE	UNIT IS A VEHICLE
1	**No Effect:** The unit being attacked gets out of the way of the lumbering herd. The attack has no effect.	**No Effect:** The unit being attacked gets out of the way of the lumbering herd. The attack has no effect.
2-5	**Look Out:** Each model from the unit must pass an Initiative test or suffer a Strength 6 AP4 hit.	**Smash!:** Each vehicle in the target unit suffers a penetrating hit.
6	**Overrun:** The target unit is destroyed.	**Flipped:** Each vehicle in the target unit scatters D6" and then suffers an Explodes! result.

LAST REPORT, BIOLOGIS SURVEY ON PYTHOSIAN XENOS MEGA FAUNA

Pythos is home to innumerable predators, ranging in size from the tiny to the gargantuan. The smallest predator we encountered was the orifice wasp, which enters the victim through an open orifice, and once ensconced within inflicts vicious and quickly lethal stings. It then feeds at leisure on the corpse. The largest beasts were the land dragon and megaloshark, both capable of swallowing a man whole.

Sadly, our survey will have to be called to a premature halt; of the 100 biotechnologists that accompanied me to Pythos, I am now the only one that remains alive. Half our number died on the first field trip, before we had catalogued a single creature! Even now I can hear the approach of a pack of spined howlerbeasts and know that my chances of leaving this fecund hell are nil...

DELVER-STRONGHOLD

Abaddon set about capturing the delver-strongholds, one by one. Black Legion warbands and hordes of daemonic creatures would capture the nearby mountain peaks, from where they could pour fire on the defenders, before making a final assault.

THE ARMIES

Select two armies using the rules found in the Fighting an Apocalypse Battle section (Apoc. pg 18). One army must be composed only of Imperial units, and the other composed only of Chaos Space Marines and Chaos Daemons units. Each side must select one of their Warlords to be their force's Warmaster.

DEPLOYMENT

The Imperial side deploys their entire army. Imperial units may be deployed on any table at least 18" from a Chaos table edge, or held in Strategic Reserve. At least one unit must be deployed on each table, and no more than a quarter of the units in the army may be deployed on a single table.

The Chaos side deploys second. Units must deploy with all models within 12" of a Chaos table edge, or be kept in Strategic Reserve. No more than half of the units in the army may deploy on a single table. Chaos units that Deep Strike can do so on any table.

After both sides have deployed, Infiltrators may deploy and Scouts redeploy using their special rules.

FIRST TURN

The Chaos side has the first turn, unless the Imperial side Seize the Initiative (Apoc. pg 22).

GAME LENGTH

The battle continues until the time limit is reached (Apoc. pg 21).

VICTORY CONDITIONS

The side that has the most Strategic Victory Points at the end of the game wins the battle (Apoc. pg 22). If both sides have an equal number of points then the battle is a draw.

MISSION SPECIAL RULES

Divine Intervention, Finest Hour, Mysterious Objectives, Strategic Assets, Strategic Objectives, Strategic Reserves, Strategic Victory Points (Apoc. pg 22-37).

Capture the Stronghold: One Strategic Objective (Apoc. pg 20) must be set up on each table. In an exception to the normal rules, they may be set up within 12" of a table edge.

Firing between Peaks: Units may fire from one table at targets that are on another table.

Moving Between the Peaks: Units may move from one table to another table during a break. In order to do so, the table the unit is moving from must not contain any enemy models. The unit will enter as if from Strategic Reserve, on the connected table edge.

Pandorax War Zone: All of the rules of engagement from the Pandorax War Zone apply to this battle.

THE BATTLEFIELD

The battle is fought on six tables as a multi-table game (Apoc. pg 54-55). Three tables must be 6' by 4' (high plateaus), and three 4' by 4' (mountain-peaks). The white arrows show where and how units can move from table to table. The smaller tables are where the delver-stronghold settlements are located, and must have suitable terrain to represent the strongholds. Finally, Strategic Objectives are placed (see Capture the Stronghold above).

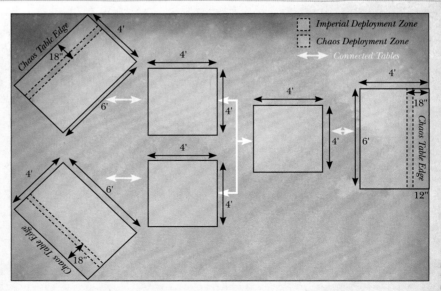

DAEMONIC APOCALYPSE

It quickly became apparent to Commander Azrael that he would need to assault the seat of Abaddon's regime at Atika and re-seal the Damnation Cache if he was ever to halt the Chaos invasion of Pythos. The initial stages of the offensive went well, but then, suddenly, a massive horde of Daemons poured forth to attack the Imperial landing site.

THE ARMIES

Select two armies using the rules found in the Fighting an Apocalypse Battle section (Apoc. pg 18). One army must be composed only of Imperial units, and the other composed only of Chaos Space Marines and Chaos Daemons units. Each side must select one of their Warlords to be their force's Warmaster.

DEPLOYMENT

The Imperial side deploys first. Imperial units can be deployed anywhere in their deployment area, or may be kept in Strategic Reserve (Apoc. pg 37).

The Chaos side deploys second. Chaos units may deploy anywhere in their deployment area that is more than 12" away from any Imperial deployment zone, or may be kept in Strategic Reserves.

After both sides have deployed, Infiltrators may deploy and Scouts redeploy using their special rules.

FIRST TURN

The Chaos side has the first turn, unless the Imperial side Seize the Initiative (Apoc. pg 22).

GAME LENGTH

The battle continues until the time limit is reached (Apoc. pg 21).

VICTORY CONDITIONS

The side that has the most Strategic Victory Points at the end of the game wins the battle (Apoc. pg 22). In the case of a tie, the Imperial side wins the battle.

MISSION SPECIAL RULES

Divine Intervention, Finest Hour, Mysterious Objectives, Strategic Assets, Strategic Objectives, Strategic Reserves, Strategic Victory Points, (Apoc. pg 22-37).

Attack-defence: Strategic Objectives in the Imperial side's deployment zone are worth double Strategic Victory Points throughout the game (Apoc. pg 22).

Death From Above: The Warmaster of the Imperial side may use one Orbital Strike shooting attack in each of their turns.

	Range	S	AP	Type
Orbital Strike	Infinite	10/8/6	1/4/-	Ordnance 1, Apocalyptic Mega-blast

Pandorax War Zone: All of the rules of engagement from the Pandorax War Zone apply to this battle.

Daemonic Apocalypse: The Warpstorm Breach Unnatural Disaster must be used when playing this mission (Apoc. pg 39). A player from the Chaos side is always the Master of Disaster (randomly choose which one each game turn).

THE BATTLEFIELD

Set up the terrain for the battle in any mutually agreeable manner and then roll-off. The winning side divides the playing area into two roughly equal halves. The border between the two halves does not have to be a straight line. The opposing side decides which half of the table each side will deploy in. Finally, Strategic Objectives are placed (Apoc. pg 20).

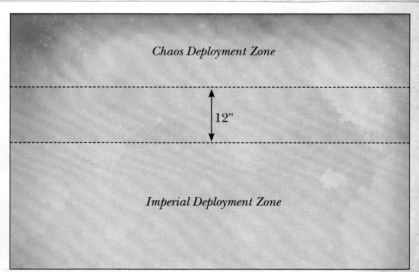

Chaos Deployment Zone

12"

Imperial Deployment Zone

THE UNDERGROUND WAR

The Damnation Cache was hidden far below Pythos' capital city, Atika, and could only be reached through a network of tunnels and caverns. When the Imperium recaptured Atika, Imperial forces were forced to battle their way through the tunnels in order to reseal the Cache.

THE ARMIES

Select two armies using the rules found in the Fighting an Apocalypse Battle section (Apoc. pg 18). One army must be composed only of Imperial units, and the other composed only of Chaos Space Marines and Chaos Daemons units. Each side must select one of their Warlords to be their force's Warmaster.

DEPLOYMENT

The Chaos side deploys first. Chaos units can be deployed anywhere on the table that is more than 30" away from a marker placed by the Imperial side (see The Battlefield, below), or may be kept in Strategic Reserve (Apoc. pg 37).

The Imperial side deploys second. Imperial units must be placed within 18" of one of the markers they placed, or may be placed in Strategic Reserve.

After both sides have deployed, Infiltrators may deploy and Scouts redeploy using their special rules.

FIRST TURN

The Imperial side has the first turn, unless the Chaos side Seize the Initiative (Apoc. pg 22).

GAME LENGTH

The battle continues until the time limit is reached (Apoc. pg 21).

VICTORY CONDITIONS

The side that has the most Strategic Victory Points at the end of the game wins the battle (Apoc. pg 22). If both sides have an equal number of points then the battle is a draw.

MISSION SPECIAL RULES

Divine Intervention, Finest Hour, Mysterious Objectives, Strategic Assets, Strategic Objectives, Strategic Reserves, Strategic Victory Points (Apoc. pg 22-37).

Pandorax War Zone: All of the rules of engagement from the Pandorax War Zone apply to this battle (mutated forms of jungle terrain are found in the tunnels and caverns.)

Reached By Tunnels: Both sides' Strategic Reserves must enter play through the tunnel markers their side set up at the start of the battle (Deep Strike may not be used). Measure the unit's first move from the marker. In addition, Flyers must pass a Dangerous Terrain test before they deploy. If the test is failed, the Flyer loses D3 Hull Points instead of being Immobilised. Then, the Flyer enters the table through one of their side's tunnel markers. Any Flyer forced to move off a table edge is destroyed.

Stone Sky: Attacks delivered by orbiting spacecraft or long-range (off-table) artillery batteries may not be used.

THE BATTLEFIELD

The battlefield represents one of the large caverns below Atika, best represented by a gaming table covered with appropriately subterranean scenery. The edges of the table represent the cavern walls.

Set up a marker at the centre of each table edge. Roll-off to see which side places the first marker, and then alternate placing them. **Each marker represents a large tunnel entering the cavern,** and determines where each side can deploy. Finally, Strategic Objectives are placed (Apoc. pg 20).

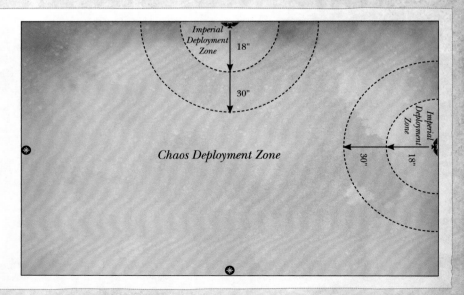

DEATH TO THE FALSE EMPEROR!

CHAOS SPACE MARINES

The warriors of the Black Legion are the Imperium's most implacable foes.

Play this card at the start of any turn. All friendly Black Legion Infantry units have the **Furious Charge** and **Hatred (Imperial)** special rules until the start of their next turn.

WAR ZONE
PANDORAX
959.M41

KREATOR REX

CHAOS SPACE MARINES

Kreator Rex's war machines led every assault on the delver-strongholds.

Play this card after deployment is complete. All friendly Chaos Space Marines Super-heavy vehicles, Super-heavy Walkers, and Super-heavy Flyers have one extra Hull Point.

WAR ZONE
PANDORAX
959.M41

RAIDERS FROM THE MAELSTROM

CHAOS SPACE MARINES

Red Corsairs warbands appear suddenly, surprising the enemy.

Play this card at the start of any turn. Any friendly Red Corsairs units that Deep Strike, or are in a Transport that Deep Strikes, have the **Shrouded** special rule until the start of their next turn.

WAR ZONE
PANDORAX
959.M41

CHAOS GATE

CHAOS DAEMONS

A Chaos gate allows Daemons to move to the material realm.

Play this card after deployment is complete, and place a Chaos Gate marker anywhere on the battlefield. Friendly Chaos Daemons units that Deep Strike will not scatter as long as the first model is placed within 12" of the marker.

WAR ZONE
PANDORAX
959.M41

THE DAMNATION CACHE

CHAOS DAEMONS

A portal to the Warp, out of which streamed hordes of Daemons.

Play this card at the start of any break. D3 units of friendly Chaos Daemons that have been completely destroyed are replaced and added to your Ongoing Reserves, following the rules for Strategic Reinforcements in the *Apocalypse* rulebook, but at no cost in Strategic Victory Points.

WAR ZONE
PANDORAX
959.M41

COLONEL STRIKE

IMPERIAL GUARD

Colonel Strike was instrumental in defeating the Chaos incursion.

Play this card during deployment to upgrade one Imperial Guard Company Commander to Colonel Strike. He has the **Fleshbane** and **Tank Hunter** special rules, and can issue up to four orders each turn.

WAR ZONE
PANDORAX
959.M41

JUNGLE AMBUSH

IMPERIAL GUARD

In their environment, Catachan Jungle Fighters are masters of concealment.

Play this card during deployment. Put up to 5 friendly Catachan Jungle Fighter Infantry units to one side. The units may be deployed in jungle terrain, more than 6" from enemy models, at the start of any of their side's turns. All units must deploy at the same time, and can move shoot and assault on the turn they arrive.

WAR ZONE
PANDORAX
959.M41

INTRACTABLE

DARK ANGELS

The Dark Angels are a ferociously stubborn foe that will never surrender.

Play this card at the start of any turn. All friendly Dark Angels units have the **Fearless** and **Relentless** special rules until the start of their next turn.

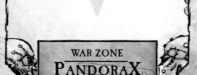

WAR ZONE
PANDORAX
959.M41

DEFY THE DAEMON

GREY KNIGHTS

The presence of the Grey Knights is anathema to Daemon-kind.

Play this card at the start of any turn. All enemy Chaos Daemons units must re-roll successful invulnerable saves of a 6 until the start of the next turn.

WAR ZONE
PANDORAX
959.M41

PANDORAX FINEST HOURS

If the following special characters are included in an army, and are one of the army's Warlords or its Warmaster, then they use the following special rules when they take their Finest Hour. These special rules are in addition to the normal benefits of a Finest Hour (Apoc. pg 26).

HORUS' SUCCESSOR
ABADDON THE DESPOILER

In the minds of the Chaos Space Marines, Abaddon's many successes are an undeniable sign of the Chaos Gods' favour, and he is seen by many as the natural successor to Horus.

If Abaddon The Despoiler calls his Finest Hour at the beginning of any turn that the opposing side has less Strategic Victory Points than Abaddon's side, the following applies.

In addition to the usual effects, he and all friendly units from *Codex: Chaos Space Marines* within 24" of him have the **Zealot** special rule.

CERTAIN DEATH
COLONEL 'DEATH' STRIKE

Colonel Strike's opponents said that fighting against him and his men when their backs were to the wall meant only one thing – certain death to whoever dared the Colonel's wrath.

If Colonel Strike calls his Finest Hour at the beginning of any turn in which the opposing side has more Strategic Victory Points than Colonel Strike's side, the following applies.

In addition to the usual effects, he and all friendly units from *Codex: Imperial Guard* within 12" of him have the **Shred** special rule.

A BEACON OF HOPE
AZRAEL

Whenever he take to the field of battle, Supreme Grand Master Azrael stands as a shining beacon of hope to his comrades and a daunting vision of holy terror to his foes.

If Azrael is within 18" of a model from either *Codex: Chaos Daemons*, or *Codex: Chaos Space Marines* when he calls his Finest Hour, the following applies.

In addition to the usual effects, Azrael has the **Fear** special rule. Furthermore, he and all friendly units within 24" of him have the **Counter-attack** and **Fearless** special rules.

CHAOS SPACE MARINES
THE CHOSEN OF ABADDON

The Chosen Chaos Space Marines that accompany Abaddon into battle include Traitor Legionnaires that are amongst the most deadly warriors in the galaxy. Each unit of the Chosen of Abaddon is led by a champion who is in his own right a Lord of Chaos, and who has found the favour of the Chaos Gods. Amongst their ranks are warriors whose names strike terror across the Imperium, such as Devram Korda, the Tyrant of Sarora, and the Chaos Sorcerer Ygethmor the Deceiver. These champions now serve Abaddon in return for the vast power that only his patronage can bring. Bound together by their lord's iron will, the Chosen of Abaddon include warriors that were once hated rivals, but now fight fearlessly to protect the Despoiler and do his bidding.

 3-5 Chaos Lords or Sorcerers

 1 unit of Chosen or Chaos Terminators for each Chaos Lord or Sorceror

FORMATION RESTRICTIONS

The units of Chosen and Chaos Terminators do not include a Champion, and therefore may have a maximum of 9 models each. Each Chaos Lord or Sorcerer must join a different unit of Chosen or Chaos Terminators, and may not leave that unit during the battle – in effect, one character takes the place of each unit's champion. The character and the unit they join must have the same Mark of Chaos, or both must have no Mark of Chaos.

SPECIAL RULES:

Blessed By The Chaos Gods: Each Chaos Lord or Sorcerer starts the battle with one Chaos Boon. Roll separately for each character when they are deployed on the battlefield.

Protect The Despoiler: Any unit from the formation within 12" of Abaddon The Despoiler has the **Fearless** special rule.

CHAOS SPACE MARINES
Daemon Engine Pack

The Forgefiends and Maulerfiends created by Chaos Warpsmiths are amongst their most prized possessions, and they only rarely commit more than one to a specific battle. Sometimes, though, when the rewards are great enough, they are willing to release all of their carefully hoarded Daemon Engines as a single force. A Daemon Engine Pack is almost always tasked with capturing an artefact that the Warpsmith desires for his own use. The pack is given the scent of the artefact's owner and are sent to hunt him down. The Warpsmith's unholy creations thunder across the battlefield, charging headlong towards the unfortunate individual, before ripping him limb from limb in order to possess the artefact the Warpsmith covets.

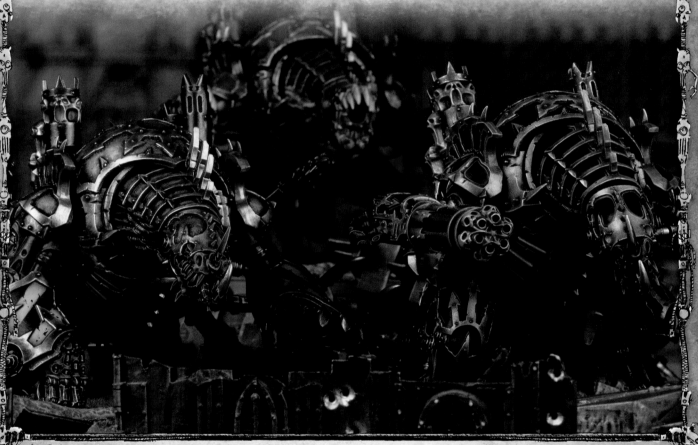

3-5 Forgefiends or Maulerfiends (in any combination)

FORMATION RESTRICTIONS
None.

SPECIAL RULES:

Hunting Pack: After deployment, but before the first turn, nominate one character model in the enemy army. All vehicles in the spearhead have the **Preferred Enemy** special rule when attacking this model. In addition, if the nominated enemy model is destroyed, the side this formation belongs to scores 1 Strategic Victory Point.

Prized Possessions: At the start of the battle, you may nominate one Chaos Warpsmith in the same army to be the Daemon Engine Pack's owner. Any models from this formation that are within 12" of the owner may use his Weapon Skill and Ballistic Skill instead of their own.

Thunderous Charge: If the spearhead is in Rapier Attack Pattern, it may charge even if it Ran in the Shooting phase.

GREAT BRASS SCORPION OF KHORNE

Brass Scorpions crawl effortlessly over all manner of terrain, unleashing a formidable array of weaponry to scour enemies from defended positions. A Brass Scorpion is nigh unstoppable, with its innate daemonic resilience transmuting an iron and brass body into an unholy substance capable of shrugging off the heaviest ordnance. Nor can a Brass Scorpion easily be halted by psychic attacks, for Khorne loathes perfidious sorcery, and powerful runes of warding protect each of his Daemon Engines.

			Armour							
GREAT BRASS SCORPION	WS	BS	S	F	S	R	I	A	HP	
	3	3	10	14	13	10	3	6	9	

700 Points
Unit Type: Super-heavy Walker
Unit Composition: 1 Great Brass Scorpion

WARGEAR:
- Demolisher cannon
- Two hellmaw cannons
- Scorpion cannon
- Daemonic possession

SPECIAL RULES:
Daemon, Daemonforge, Fleet, It Will Not Die.

Doomsday Reactor: The Great Brass Scorpion suffers a +2 modifier to any rolls made for it on the Catastrophic Damage table.

Runes of the Blood God: Any Psyker that targets the Great Brass Scorpion with a psychic power automatically suffers Perils of the Warp, regardless of whether or not they pass their Psychic test. If they happen to roll a double 1 or double 6, the Psyker also suffers Terrors of the Warp (Apoc. pg 65).

	Range	S	AP	Type
Demolisher cannon	24"	10	2	Ordnance 1, Large Blast
Hellmaw cannon	Template	6	3	Assault 1
Scorpion cannon	36"	6	3	Heavy 10

WAR ZONE
PANDORAX
959.M41

THE HOUNDS OF HURON

The Hounds of Huron are the harbingers of Lord Huron Blackheart's dark fury. They use their speed to hunt down prey, lashing out with roaring chainswords and slashing with scythed blades. Biker squads are ideally suited to hit and run raids, the destruction of isolated targets, or the tracking and execution of fleeing enemies. Large squadrons of Chaos Bikers provide a violent and destructive force, although they tend only to group together under the command of a particularly powerful Chaos Lord. It takes an individual who can promise the renegades an even greater bounty to temporarily gain their allegiance. Huron's Huntmasters are men such as this, imposing figures in the Red Corsairs' vanguard who answer only to Lord Blackheart himself.

1 Chaos Lord

5+ Chaos Biker squads

FORMATION RESTRICTIONS
The Chaos Lord must take a Chaos bike.

SPECIAL RULES:
Acute Senses, Outflank.

Lightning Strike: The Chaos Lord, and all other units in the formation within 12" of him, may charge even if they have Turbo-boosted during that turn.

CHAOS SPACE MARINES
KHORNE TOWER OF SKULLS

Hammered out of arcane brass and iron at the foot of the Blood God's throne and infused with the essence of countless damned souls, each Tower of Skulls is the equivalent of a small and terrible army in its own right. There are sixty-four Towers of Skulls, each one named for an aspect of Khorne's beloved bloodletting. Legend tells that they roam the great arid wastes before the Blood God's citadel, firing their bellowing cannons to reap the lives of enemy and ally alike in Khorne's unholy name. Only by felling the Tower of Skulls can the foe hope to claim victory, yet this is no simple task. Each soul claimed by the Tower of Skulls infuses it with unholy power, allowing it to reknit even the most catastrophic damage.

KHORNE TOWER OF SKULLS	BS	F	S	R	HP
	4	14	13	12	9

750 Points

Unit Type: Super-heavy vehicle
Unit Composition: 1 Tower of Skulls

WARGEAR:
- Balemaw cannon
- Two doomfire cannons
- Two skullreaper cannons
- Two twin-linked skullshredders

SPECIAL RULES:
Daemon, Daemonforge, It Will Not Die.

Doomsday Reactor: The Khorne Tower of Skulls suffers a +2 modifier to any rolls made for it on the Catastrophic Damage table.

Reknit Form: The Khorne Tower of Skulls recovers one lost Hull Point for every 10 unsaved Wounds it inflicts in a single phase.

Runes of the Blood God: Any Psyker that targets the Khorne Tower of Skulls with a psychic power automatically suffers Perils of the Warp, regardless of whether or not they pass their Psychic test. If they happen to roll a double 1 or double 6, the Psyker they also suffer Terrors of the Warp (Apoc. pg 65).

	Range	S	AP	Type
Balemaw cannon	60"	9	3	Primary Weapon 1, Apocalyptic Blast
Doomfire cannon	24"	4	4	Heavy 2, Large Blast
Skullreaper cannon	36"	6	3	Heavy 6
Skullshredder	24"	4	4	Heavy 5

CHAOS SPACE MARINES
MAELSTROM OF GORE

In times of great moment, when the warbands of the World Eaters Legion are mustered for war, the high priests of Khorne call upon their patron's favour. With a deafening crack of thunder like the warcry of Khorne himself, the skies open and blood rains down in great squalls. A storm of gore spatters and soaks all those who would stand in the path of the World Eaters' rampage. When they can hold back no more, the berzerker warriors of Khorne run screaming into the ranks of their prey. The ensorcelled lifeblood hammering down from the skies invigorates the psychotic warriors of the Blood God and drives them on to ever more extravagant acts of butchery. Chainaxes rise and fall in bloody arcs as the defenders arrayed against the World Eaters are hewn and cut apart in their hundreds.

 OR 1 Chaos Lord or
Khârn the Betrayer

8 units of Khorne Berzerkers

FORMATION RESTRICTIONS
If a Chaos Lord is taken, he must have the Mark of Khorne. Each unit of Khorne Berzerkers must have at least 8 models.

SPECIAL RULES:
Slick with Ensorcelled Blood: If a unit from this formation is within 18" of the Chaos Lord leading them (or Khârn the Betrayer if he is in this formation), it has the **Fleet** and **Move Through Cover** special rules and adds 3" to its charge move.

'KILL! MAIM! BURN! KILL! MAIM! BURN!'

– KHÂRN THE BETRAYER

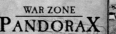

CHAOS SPACE MARINES
PLAGUEREAPER OF NURGLE

The Plaguereaper super-heavy tank is a half-corroded bastion amongst the forces of Nurgle – a gurgling, miasma-clouded fortress of pestilence. Huge vats of virulent slime distilled from rotting, plague-ridden corpses are mounted on the back of the vehicle, feeding through bulging pipes into the main turret. The Plaguereaper's pus cannon squirts out this horrendous concoction, dousing swathes of enemy troops who are ensured a most hideous death as their skin instantly erupts in weeping boils and their flesh is eaten away from within. Anyone foolish enough to assault this stinking behemoth is assailed by the hordes of Nurglings that infest its internal spaces and cling to its hull. Truly, this is one of the most unpleasant engines of war an enemy can face.

PLAGUEREAPER OF NURGLE	BS	Armour			HP
		F	S	R	
	4	14	13	12	9

575 Points
Unit Type: Super-heavy vehicle
Unit Composition: 1 Plaguereaper

WARGEAR:

- Demolisher cannon
- Pus cannon
- Two lascannons (sponson)
- Three twin-linked heavy bolters (two sponson, one hull)
- Searchlight
- Smoke launchers

OPTIONS:

- May take any of the following:
  - Havoc launcher...10 pts
  - Pintle-mounted twin-linked bolter or combi-flamer..10 pts

SPECIAL RULES:

Nurgling Infestation: Any unit that attacks the Plaguereaper in the Fight sub-phase suffers 3D6 Strength 3 AP- hits at Initiative step 3 (even if the Plaguereaper is destroyed at an earlier Initiative step).

	Range	S	AP	Type
Pus cannon	Hellstorm	7	3	Primary Weapon 1
Demolisher cannon	24"	10	2	Ordnance 1, Large Blast
Heavy bolter	36"	5	4	Heavy 3
Lascannon	48"	9	2	Heavy 1

CHAOS SPACE MARINES
TRINITY OF BLOOD

Summoned through the exsanguination of worlds and the offering of skulls beyond counting, a Trinity of Blood is a physical embodiment of the rage in Khorne's molten heart. Comprised of three Lords of Skulls united in their hate for all natural things, the very ground is gouged at a Trinity's thunderous advance to reveal cracks awash with boiling blood and jetting flames. A cloud of furious emotion billows before the Trinity, its inescapable vapours driving those who breath it to spill blood for the Blood God. Any who die well in the ensuing carnage are judged worthy, their skulls gathered for Khorne's Throne by the Lords of Skulls themselves.

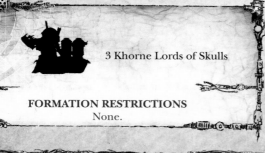

3 Khorne Lords of Skulls

FORMATION RESTRICTIONS
None.

'Only the insane have strength enough to prosper.'

SPECIAL RULES:

Cloud of Fury: All non-vehicle models (friend or foe) within 12" of one or more models from the Trinity of Blood at the beginning of the Assault phase, have the **Rage** special rule for the remainder of that phase.

Wounds in the World: Once per game, at the beginning of the enemy's Movement phase, the Trinity of Blood may open wounds in the ground beneath the foe. Each enemy model that starts their Movement phase within 24" of a model from this formation must take a Dangerous Terrain test. Units with the Flyer, Super-heavy Flyer, Skimmer, Jetbike, Flying Monstrous Creature, Flying Gargantuan Creature, Jet Pack or Jump unit type are not affected by this rule.

CHAOS DAEMONS
DAEMONIC FORGEHOST

When the Forge of Souls sends forth its Soul Grinders in great Forgehosts, a few of its minions are made into Keepers of the Forge. These chosen Soul Grinders are gifted with powerful psychosonic devices, similar to the warhorns carried by their daemonic brethren. The cacophonous blare of these supernatural instruments allows the Keepers to act as a focus, guiding the other Soul Grinders in the host through the currents of the Warp as they break into reality. The guidance provided by the Keeper of the Forge makes the transition between the Immaterium and reality considerably easier. In turn, this allows the host of the Daemon Forge to jump on their enemies in the very same moment that they appear out of the ether.

 3-5 Soul Grinders

FORMATION RESTRICTIONS
None.

SPECIAL RULES:

Daemonic Guide: The Daemonic Forgehost enters play by Deep Strike. To do so, first Deep Strike the Command Vehicle as normal, then simply deploy all the other Soul Grinders in the spearhead within 6" of the Command Vehicle (do not roll for scatter).

Forge On!: All Soul Grinders in this formation, except for the Command Vehicle, can charge in the turn they deploy.

IMPERIAL GUARD
DEATHSTRIKE VORTEX MISSILE BATTERY

Of all the weapons in the Imperial arsenal, few are feared as much as a Deathstrike Vortex Missile Battery. The plasma warheads on the Deathstrike missiles in the battery are replaced with rare vortex warheads. Even a single vortex warhead is capable of destroying a battle formation; three or more can lay waste to an army or destroy an entire city.

 3-5 Deathstrike Missile Launchers

FORMATION RESTRICTIONS
None.

SPECIAL RULES:

Battery Fire: Models in this formation are not equipped with deathstrike missiles and do not use the T-Minus Five Minutes to Launch... and Counting special rule. Instead, one vortex missile may be fired by a vehicle in this formation each game turn, starting from game turn two. You may choose to delay the firing of any missile until any future game turn if you prefer. For example, if you do not fire a missile on game turn 2, you may fire two missiles on game turn 3. Vortex missiles have the following profile:

	Range	S	AP	Type
Vortex missile	12"-960"	D	1	Ordnance 1, Highly Volatile, Large Blast, Vortex, One use only

Highly Volatile: If a vehicle in the spearhead suffers a Weapon Destroyed result before it has fired its vortex missile, then the missile explodes on the launcher. The vehicle is destroyed, and a vortex is created with the profile above, centred on the point that the vehicle occupied.

IMPERIAL GUARD
'EMPEROR'S MERCY' COMMISSARIAT SQUAD

A Commissariat Squad is deployed when casualty rates are expected to be particularly high. In theory, the presence of an elite cadre of the Departmento Munitorum's officers should rouse the men to deeds of great courage and valour; in practise, the men they accompany are so fearful of the Commissariat that they throw themselves into the thickest fighting to avoid any suspicion of cowardice.

1 Lord Commissar

3+ Commissars

FORMATION RESTRICTIONS
None.

SPECIAL RULES:
Fearless.

Pinpoint Execution: If a friendly Imperial Guard squad fails a Morale test within 12" of this unit, follow the rules for Summary Execution as if a Commissar was in that squad.

Show Them the Emperor's Mercy!: The range of the Lord Commissar's Aura of Discipline is increased to 12", and any friendly Imperial Guard unit within this range – including the formation itself – has the **Furious Charge** and **Hatred** special rules.

STORM TROOPER MISSION ELITE

Storm Troopers are one of the most valuable resources available to Imperial Commanders. Their deployment en masse is rare, usually involving the completion of a vital mission that cannot be entrusted to lesser men. Such formations invariably deploy via fast-moving wings of Valkyries, relying on brutal efficiency and the element of surprise to storm and secure their allotted objective.

2+ Storm Trooper Squads

FORMATION RESTRICTIONS

All Storm Trooper squads must take a Valkyrie as a Dedicated Transport.

SPECIAL RULES:

Storm the Objective: In any turn in which a unit of Storm Troopers from this formation disembarks from its Valkyrie, it may shoot, Run, and then shoot again. This second set of shooting attacks may be at a different target if you wish. In addition, for the duration of this turn, all shooting attacks made by this squad (but not their Valkyrie) have the **Ignores Cover** special rule.

Vital Mission: At the beginning of the first turn, nominate one Strategic Objective in the enemy deployment zone. At the end of each scheduled session of play, if a unit from the Storm Trooper Mission Elite controls this objective, it is worth an additional Strategic Victory Point.

WAR ZONE
PANDORAX
959.M41

IMPERIAL GUARD
TRAITOR'S BANE

Colonel Strike of the Catachan 183rd has become legendary for two things – his inspirational leadership during the Pandorax campaign, and his personalised Hellhammer super-heavy tank, Traitor's Bane. Tired of waiting for armoured reinforcements that he suspected would never come, Strike had his field engineers rebuild a ruined Hellhammer they found in the jungle from the ground up. Impact dampeners and engine muffles were installed, broad-spectrum and native camouflage systems were applied, synched heavy flamers were loaded with pressurized promethium. The resultant super-tank formed Strike's command bunker for the rest of the campaign, an armoured behemoth capable of moving unseen through Pandorax's jungle until it was too late for the foe to escape.

TRAITOR'S BANE	BS	F	S	R	HP
	3	14	13	12	9

750 Points

Unit Type: Super-heavy vehicle
Unit Composition: Traitor's Bane

WARGEAR:
- Autocannon
- Demolisher cannon
- Hellhammer cannon
- Four lascannons (sponson)
- Twin-linked heavy bolter
- Four synched heavy flamers (sponson)
- Searchlight
- Smoke launchers

	Range	S	AP	Type
Hellhammer cannon	36"	10	1	Primary Weapon 1, Massive Blast, Ignores Cover
Autocannon	48"	7	4	Heavy 2
Demolisher cannon	24"	10	2	Ordnance 1, Large Blast
Heavy bolter	36"	5	4	Heavy 3
Lascannon	48"	9	2	Heavy 1
Synched heavy flamer	Template	6	3	Assault 1, Twin-linked

SPECIAL RULES:
Broad-spectrum Camouflage: *Traitor's Bane* has the **Stealth** special rule. Against Flyers, Super-heavy Flyers, Flying Monstrous Creatures and Flying Gargantuan Creatures, it instead has the **Shrouded** special rule.

'What manner of fool would deny the Emperor's Will?'

Xerxes Airborne Support Wing

A Xerxes Airborne Support Wing consists of three to five Valkyrie assault carriers that have been specially modified so that they can loose a fearsome barrage of missiles with their multiple rocket pods. Their cargo bays are filled with additional ammunition for the rocket pods, which allows the Valkyries to ripple fire their rockets, swathing a huge area of ground with high explosive fire.

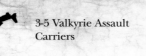

3-5 Valkyrie Assault Carriers

FORMATION RESTRICTIONS

All models in this formation must be equipped with multiple rocket pods.

SPECIAL RULES:

Ammunition Stowage: The Valkyries in this formation have a Transport Capacity of 0.

Fire of Xerxes: Two or more models in the formation can combine their multiple rocket pod attacks into a single attack with the profile below each turn. All participating models must be in range and have line of sight to the target.

Range	S	AP	Type
72"	4+X	6	Heavy X, Apocalyptic Barrage, Ripple Fire

Ripple Fire: X is equal to the number of Valkyries that are participating in the Fire of Xerxes shooting attack.

MARAUDER BOMBER

Sturdily built, and boasting a colossal payload for its size, the Marauder is the archetypal heavy bomber of the Imperium. Like all Imperial aircraft, Marauders come under the command of the Imperial Navy, and are often based on orbiting spacecraft, as they can operate in the vacuum of space. While a Marauder is considered capable of all manner of strike missions, it is most commonly employed as an interdiction aircraft. Squadrons of Marauders fly deep into enemy territory and attack supply dumps, troop convoys and other targets of opportunity. Such is the ordnance at each Marauder's disposal that a single aircraft is capable of chewing a column of infantry into sheer bloody ruin within seconds of its target registering the tell-tale drone of the Marauder's engines.

		Armour						385 Points
	BS	F	S	R	HP			**Unit Type:** Super-heavy Flyer
MARAUDER BOMBER	3	10	10	10	9			**Unit Composition:** 1 Marauder Bomber

WARGEAR:
- Two twin-linked heavy bolters
- Twin-linked lascannon
- Two Marauder bomb racks

OPTIONS:
- May replace its two Marauder bomb racks with two hellstorm bombs .... *free*

	Range	S	AP	Type
Heavy bolter	36"	5	4	Heavy 3
Hellstorm bomb	–	7	3	Bomb, Apocalyptic Blast, Ignores Cover, One use only
Lascannon	48"	9	2	Heavy 1
Marauder bomb rack	–	6	4	Bomb, Apocalyptic Barrage 6, One use only

Bomb: The rules for bombing runs are found in the *Warhammer 40,000* rulebook.

IMPERIUM
WARHOUND HUNTING PACK

Warhound Titans usually hunt in pairs that are known as hunting packs. Dozens of these packs will range ahead of a Titan Legion, scouting out the enemy and tracking their movements. Although small by the standards of a Battle Titan, a pair of Warhounds are perfectly capable of dealing with most opponents that they may meet on the battlefield. One will distract the enemy with long range fire, pinning them down while the second bounds forward. Once the second Warhound is in position, it will unleash a hail of fire that will allow its pack brother to move forward in its turn. Bounding forward in this manner, one after the other, the two Warhounds can easily outmanoeuvre any foe, driving them from cover and catching them in a deadly crossfire.

2 Warhound Titans

FORMATION RESTRICTIONS
None.

SPECIAL RULES:
Scouts.

Covering Fire: If both models in this formation are within 12" of each other, they both have the **Shrouded** special rule.

Crossfire: If a Warhound from this formation shoots at a unit that has already been targeted by the other Warhound this phase, then any successful cover saves against its shooting attacks must be re-rolled.

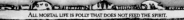

ALL MORTAL LIFE IS FOLLY THAT DOES NOT FEED THE SPIRIT.

DARK ANGELS
TALON OF VENGEANCE

The Ravenwing is a rapid response force, and because of this, it is the first of the Dark Angels Companies to follow up a rumour of the Fallen's presence. Should a coven of such individuals muster together on the same planet, they will usually have massed armies under their sway. In such times are the Talons of Vengeance employed – Dark Talon squadrons and their Nephilim escorts that can plummet out of orbit at the bark of a single vox-cast, swooping on the coordinates supplied and dropping their stasis bombs in synchronicity so the Fallen are held frozen in time, ripe for collection. Though the combined stasis field is powerful, its duration is no longer than a few seconds – and yet it provides time enough for the Deathwing to close in on the enemy and complete the job.

2-4 Ravenwing Dark Talons

1 Nephilim Jetfighter

FORMATION RESTRICTIONS
None.

'What is the terror of death?

That we die our work incomplete.

What is the joy of life?

To die knowing our task is done.'

SPECIAL RULES:

Stasis Prison: If an enemy unit is hit by two or more stasis bomb attacks made by Dark Talons from this formation in the same turn, then the unit becomes trapped in a Stasis Prison. Whilst trapped, it is treated as being out of play entirely – it cannot make any actions whatsoever, neither can it be shot at, charged or affected in any way. No other models may approach within 1" of a model in a Stasis Prison.

The number of phases the unit is trapped is determined from the table below and depends on the number of stasis bomb attacks that hit the target unit. Once the Stasis Prison has been in play for the appropriate number of phases, it dissipates and the unit(s) within it are free to act as normal.

NO. OF BOMBS	DURATION OF STASIS PRISON
2	Until the beginning of the opponent's next Shooting phase
3	Until the beginning of the opponent's next Assault phase
4	Until the beginning of your next Movement phase

DARK ANGELS
THUNDERHEAD SQUADRON

It is said that the Dark Angels ride to war upon the wings of the storm, and not without good reason. In times of all-consuming war, the Ravenwing will muster its darkest relics and mount them upon a squadron of Land Speeder Darkshrouds. Escorted to war by a flotilla of Land Speeders and support variants that only the Ravenwing can provide, the Darkshrouds carve through the troubled skies, the nebulous and gloomy aura of their relics magnified by their proximity to one another. As the squadron flies through hurricane and storm front, the cloud banks are drawn in their wake, a billowing wall of black fog that obscures the massed Ravenwing assault riding behind. When the Thunderhead Squadron strikes, the clouds they carry with them break to reveal their secret – destruction has come!

3 Ravenwing Darkshrouds

1+ Land Speeder Vengeance

1+ Ravenwing Support Squadron

FORMATION RESTRICTIONS
None.

SPECIAL RULES:
Scout, Shrouded.

The Thunderhead: Enemy models may not draw line of sight over or beneath a Darkshroud model in the Thunderhead Squadron, or between two Darkshroud models that are within 6" of each other. Note that line of sight can still be drawn to a Darkshroud model, but not beyond it.

GREY KNIGHTS
Assassinorum Murder Squad

There are those abroad in the galaxy so dangerous that the High Lords of Terra will employ every resource they can to bring about their destruction. In such times, all the major temples of the Officio Assassinorum will equip their best operatives with ancient and deadly relics and group them into a single murder squad. Their combined powers are a force as sure as death's own blade.

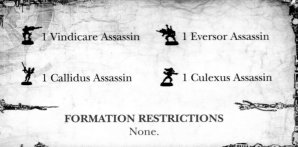

1 Vindicare Assassin 1 Eversor Assassin

1 Callidus Assassin 1 Culexus Assassin

FORMATION RESTRICTIONS
None.

SPECIAL RULES:

Best of the Best: The Assassins in a Murder Squad each have 3 Wounds, and their synskin confers the **Feel No Pain (5+)** special rule.

Black Frenzon: The Eversor's frenzon confers 2D6 extra Attacks as a charge bonus instead of 1D6.

Exitus Relics: The Vindicare's exitus weaponry has the **Soul Blaze** special rule (this affects all of their special ammunition types).

Neural Obliterator: The Callidus' neural shredder is Strength 9.

Speculum Majora: The Culexus' animus speculum is Strength 6.

APPENDIX

The Pandorax campaign was a vast conflict, fought all across the surface of the planet Pythos and in the dark depths of space in the Pandorax system itself. Providing comprehensive information on all of the combatants would take several dozen volumes at least; instead, this diverse overview concerns some of the most important formations that took part.

AN OVERVIEW OF CATACHAN JUNGLE FIGHTER REGIMENTS AND THEIR COMBAT TECHNIQUES

'Us Catachans love our world. Ain't nowhere else I'd choose to be brought up. Catachan's got but one thing for the Emperor – us. Ain't no minerals, can't build a hive world there. But you want some real tough men for your fighting, Catachan's the place to go to. You live on Catachan, you're a born survivor. Half the kids die before they learn to walk. Half of those that walk won't see ten years. But you celebrate your tenth birthday, you're gonna be a real man.'

Catachan is a planet so inimical to life that every day there is a battle for survival. As the most infamous death world in the galaxy, Catachan has a fearsome reputation, and its inhabitants are the deadliest breed of jungle fighters serving the Emperor. To do battle with the warriors of Catachan is to fight the very forces of nature itself.

The hardy Catachan people are descendants of the very first settlers who colonised the planet generations ago. By necessity, they are a tough breed well versed in survival amidst planet-wide jungles that swarm with voracious predators, flesh-eating plants, poisonous insects and virulent diseases. Catachan has but one resource of value to the Imperium; their superb regiments of Jungle Fighters. Once recruited they are dispatched to war zones all across the galaxy where their skills in jungle warfare are at a premium. Catachan warriors readily accept the call to arms; in exchange for their loyalty, their families and settlements receive technologies and medicines that are otherwise impossible for them to obtain.

The leader of a Catachan company or regiment is always a respected figure amongst his men. He is often a renowned hunter or warrior, the headman of the settlement from which the company was recruited or perhaps the patriarch of an extended family which has sent many of its men-folk to join the ranks of the Guard. Discipline is maintained through trust and respect rather than by rank and Catachan Jungle Fighters take pride in the fact that their officers share with them every danger and hardship.

Catachan infantry squads make up the bulk of a jungle fighting force. Lightly equipped, they can move quickly through thick vegetation but still make use of heavy weapons when the situation demands. The squads that make up a Catachan Jungle Fighter platoon are often more independent than traditional regiments such as those of the Cadian Shock Troops or Death Korps of Krieg; each squad will move autonomously, opening fire at their sergeant's command. Jungle Fighters squads often make long range penetration raids behind enemy lines, scouting out the terrain and locating specific targets. Before the main forces engage in battle, Jungle Fighter patrols will set up ambushes and lay booby traps where they can do the most harm. In the jungle, even the slightest scratch can prove to be fatal as necrotic bacteria swarm in to putrefy it, and Catachan Jungle Fighters take advantage of these harsh conditions by rigging traps from the natural materials covering the battlefield such as vines and tree branches. They also use a variety of purpose-built devices to create 'devil's gardens' – areas where the most innocuous looking mound of leaves or tree root can conceal a shredder mine or plasma charge.

Most Catachan regiments include squads of veteran warriors exceptional even by the exacting standards of their birth world. Within the regiment, and beyond, these units are called 'Catachan Devils' in reference to their famous kill-knives and the voracious predators of their world. Formed from the bravest and hardiest of the regiment's warriors, veteran Jungle Fighter squads take the fight directly to the enemy. They bear the brunt of the bloody combat which often occurs when fighting in the close confines of the jungle and so are heavily armed with demolition charges, flamers, meltaguns and plasma weapons.

Compared to most Imperial Guard forces, Catachan regiments have few dedicated heavy weapons squads. The weapons' bulk and the weight of the ammunition they require makes them difficult to transport across a wilderness. Nonetheless, the firepower of heavy bolters and

autocannons can be decisive in close fought jungle battles. Mortars are also greatly favoured by Catachan regiments, as they have the ability to rain fire upon the foe while the Mortar crew stays far back among the enshrouding trees. This makes them an invaluable weapon because, unlike heavy bolters and autocannons, mortars can support the widely spread Catachan Veteran squads despite the close terrain. Barrages of mortars are also useful for pinning down enemy units, enabling Jungle Fighter squads to outmanoeuvre them.

Specialised sniper squads are considered every bit as important for providing supporting fire as heavy weapon squads. Catachan regiments recruit their own snipers from amongst their finest marksmen. A Catachan sniper will take up position hours, or even days, before a battle: after finding the best spot in trees or among roots, he will conceal himself fully before the enemy draws near. Concentrated sniper fire can throw enemy units into complete confusion, while the snipers themselves are almost impossible to spot in the dense jungle canopy.

The vehicles assigned to support Catachan Jungle Fighter regiments are almost always modified by the canny guardsmen to better suit fighting in a dense environment. Many bear equipment to cut through undergrowth, and almost all are swathed in camo netting embellished with choice pieces of local flora. Sentinels are particularly popular among Catachan regiments for their ability to traverse the most uneven terrain alongside the infantry. Roving hunter-killer groups of Sentinels armed with heavy flamers and sporting chainsaws are used to obliterate knots of enemy resistance.

Ogryns are also used to provide heavy support. Some Ogryns are native to Catachan, but where they are not, certain Catachan regiments will 'acquire' squads of them, often without informing their previous commanders. Catachan Veterans find Ogryns have the same values of personal loyalty, physical toughness and determination as they do themselves, so the two groups get on famously well.

CATACHAN KNIVES

'We've run into scorpions the size of battle tanks, three men died from eyerot last week, I've sweat enough to fill a lake, my boots got sucked into a sink-swamp and the trees are so thick in places, you can't squeeze between them. Emperor help me, I love this place! It's just like home!'

A knife is not only the tool and weapon of a Catachan fighter but also a mark of his status. The steel alloy used for these knives is unique to the planet Catachan. A well-honed Catachan blade will not rust and its edge will be keen even after continuous use.

Catachan knives are highly valued and sought after throughout the Imperium. Many counterfeit copies are sold by roaming rogue traders, but the only sure way to get an authentic blade is to take it from a Catachan. This is not easy, as the Catachans place a tremendous value on their knives. It is said that a Catachan would rather give up his right arm than his knife.

Each Catachan Jungle Fighter learns the craft of making knives from his parents and making your own knife is considered one of the tests of adulthood. While the basic design of these knives remain the same, there are subtle variations between different family groups and individuals, depending on the height and preferences of the user.

CATACHAN FANG

Measuring up to twenty inches of steel, the Catachan Fang is the most common type of knife used by the Catachan regiments. Equally useful for cutting your way through jungle or a deviant Eldar, the Catachan Fang is renowned throughout thousands of star systems.

This knife is also used for settling disputes between Catachans. Usually, one knife is placed in the centre of a fighting pit and the combatants must each strive to claim it. The duel ends when one fighter draws blood, though this can often mean death as well.

NIGHT REAPER

Smaller than other typical designs, the blackened blade of the Night Reaper is especially suitable for infiltration and night missions when light reflecting from a blade can mean the difference between life and death. The blade itself is triangular, so a wound caused by it is unlikely to clot or heal. Catachans are also

known to poison these knives using one of the many venoms native to their inhospitable planet, making them even more sure of a kill.

DEVIL'S CLAW

Named after the fearsome predator of the Catachan jungles, this is the largest of the traditional knives of Catachan. Anywhere between three and four feet long, the Devil's Claw is closer to a sword than a knife. It is used mainly on the battlefield in close quarters and it has even achieved a fearsome reputation amongst Orks, who call it 'Da Cutta'.

The blade itself is hollow and half filled with mercury to give it greater swinging power. The power swords wielded by the more senior members of Catachan regiments are often identical in design to the Devil's Claw.

BATTLEFLEETS OF THE IMPERIUM

The human colonisation of the galaxy owes its accomplishment to two things – the nightmarish alternate realm of Warp space, and the ships that dare travel through it. Warp space lies alongside and around the material universe, a dimension comprised solely of shifting energies and formless consciousness. In the Warp there is no time, no distance, only a constantly flowing stream of Immaterium. A starship equipped with Warp engines can break through the barrier separating the real universe from the Warp, thus removing itself from the normal flow of time. Only by traversing the Immaterium can the immense distances between stars be covered within a single lifetime, though even Warp travel is not instantaneous. Aboard a ship in the Warp a single month of perceived time may pass, yet in the material realm anything from a day to many years may have elapsed. The vagaries of the Immaterium mean that it is even posited that a craft could reach its destination before its journey began. This can mean that fleets and armies responding to calls for aid may turn up months, years or even decades too late to help and this further adds to the anarchy and confusion of conducting hundreds of wars across the whole galaxy.

It is sometimes difficult for those born under the claustrophobic sky of a planet to appreciate the antiquity and dignity which is inherent in

all old spacecraft. Most Imperial starships are old – open space, the most hostile environment to man, preserves the plastics and metals that spacecraft are made from. Space gifts them with the power to endure through generations of men. Thus starships launched during the Great Crusade are still in service in the 41st Millennium; most have, in their vast lifetimes, been refitted, modernised or reconstructed many times. Barring a major accident or destruction in battle, a ship is immortal like a great city, its population and fabric existing in a constant state of decay and renewal.

THE IMPERIAL NAVY

Almost every ship in the Imperium is part of the Imperial Fleet: the relative handful of vessels that are not belong mostly to a few powerful organisations such as the Adeptus Mechanicus, Space Marine Chapters and the Inquisition, or a small number of honoured and ancient merchant families. Even Imperial Guard regiments must rely upon the Imperial Fleet to transport them between war zones. This fleet is divided into the civilian vessels of the Merchant Fleet and the warships of the Imperial Navy.

The Imperial Navy numbers many thousands of ships, the majority of which are at least a thousand years old. Some are as old as the Imperium itself, a full ten thousand years. A very few claim a pre-Imperial origin. It is not surprising, therefore, that these craft vary tremendously in their appearance, even where they belong to the same general class or type.

To aid organisation, the Imperium is split into five Segmentae Majoris, each of which has its own merchant and naval fleet. The fleet stations for these vessels are on the Segmentum Fortress in each Segmentum – Mars for the Segmentum Solar, Kar Duniash in the Ultima Segmentum, Bakka in the Segmentum Tempestus, Hydraphur in the Segmentum Pacificus and Cypra Mundi in the Segmentum Obscurus. The Segmentum fleet commanders, the Lord High Admirals, are immensely powerful individuals.

All Imperial space is further broken down into sectors, most usually 'cubes' of space roughly 200 light years to a side. Each comprises of a number of sub-sectors centred on densely populated star clusters, important worlds, or the meeting points of trade routes. The areas between sub-sectors and sectors – unexplored or uninhabited regions, alien empires and areas inaccessible from the Warp – are known as wilderness space, and make up a far greater proportion of the galaxy than that controlled by Humanity.

For practical purposes, a sector's battlefleet is the largest operational naval organisation, under the command of its Lord Admiral. Each battlefleet is almost always divided into a number of battlegroups at any given time. These are not permanent organisations, but are instead task forces, convoy escorts, patrol flotillas and other fleets that have each been assembled to perform a specific function or series of tasks. A few battlegroups are almost permanent institutions, such as the famous 1st Terran Battlecruiser Armada, but most are gathered and then dispersed as necessity dictates, though due to the scale of the Imperium of Man, a temporary battlegroup may serve together for several decades. Depending on its size and role, a battlegroup may be commanded by an experienced ship's captain, a fleet admiral or admiral, or sometimes even the Lord Admiral himself.

IMPERIAL NAVY BATTLEFLEETS

Each Imperial Navy battlefleet normally consists of between 50 and 75 warships of varying size, although those of some sectors exceed this considerably, according to the importance of the sector and the number of enemies it must contend with. As well as these destroyers, frigates, cruisers and battleships, a battlefleet also has access to countless smaller vessels such as transports, shuttles, messenger craft and long-range patrol craft. In addition to interstellar vessels, a sector will also be protected by numerous ships incapable of Warp travel, such as system patrol ships and defence monitors. These are backed up by stationary defences – space stations, orbital defence platforms, ground-based defence lasers and missile silos and orbital mines.

This may seem like a formidable armada, and even half a dozen ships of the line possess firepower on a planetary scale, but the area each fleet is required to cover is huge and the navy must be ready to perform many varied and difficult tasks. An average sector, perhaps in one of the western spiral arms where Humanity is most dense, can contain tens of thousands of stars and cover an area of 8,000,000 cubic light years. Within this vast wilderness, only a small fraction of systems have planets and a small proportion of these will be inhabited, or indeed inhabitable. However, the ships of a battlefleet must constantly scour this boundless area for enemies; protecting merchant shipping from pirates and alien attacks, transporting and escorting Imperial Guard armies, giving orbital support for planetary invasion, not to mention providing exploration fleets and routine patrols.

SPACE MARINE FLEETS

To further advance the deadly specialisation of the Adeptus Astartes, Space Marine fleets are built for transport and planetary assault rather than fleet-on-fleet warfare. Only the smallest of vessels act exclusively as gunships, with the larger Battle Barges and Strike Cruisers remaining predominantly aids to invasion, though they are far from defenceless.

Unlike the vessels of the Imperial Navy, a Space Marine ship has a relatively small crew. A Space Marine is far too valuable to waste in manning a gun or watching a surveyor screen, and so only the officers aboard a vessel are likely to be Space Marines, as well as the few Techmarines who oversee the engines and perform other mechanical duties. Almost all the ship's systems are entrusted to servitors; half-human cyborgs wired into the vessel's weapons, engines and communications apparatus.

SHIP TYPES

The ships of the Imperium are without exception vast vessels. Even the smallest Warp-capable starship is hundreds of meters long and has thousands of crew, while the largest are kilometers long and have crews numbering in the tens of thousands. The bows and hulls of these immense craft are studded with arrays of weapons, and they are capable of devastating entire planets from orbit if need be. The ships that make up the Imperial fleet can be split into three broad categories:

Battleships (including the Battle Barges found in Space Marine fleets) are the largest fighting ships in space. They can absorb a tremendous amount of damage and mount weapons batteries capable of laying waste to entire continents. These vessels are so huge that they are comparatively slow and ponderous to manoeuvre, so they need support from other vessels to bring the enemy to battle. The commander of a sizable fleet will often lead from the helm of a battleship, for each of these behemoths sports more firepower (and thus presents a greater threat to the enemy) than any other ship under his command.

The versatile cruisers are the workhorses of any fleet. They are manoeuvrable, well-armed ships, about half the size of a battleship, and capable of operating away from a base for extended periods. This means that cruisers are used for extended patrols, blockades and raiding deep into enemy held space. In a major battle, cruisers screen the approach of the fleet in support of the escorts and form the gun line once battle begins.

Much smaller than cruisers or battleships, escort ships are the most common warships in any fleet. They usually operate in squadrons of three to five vessels. Escorts are fast, lightly armed and capable of running rings around heavier ships, which they accompany to protect them against torpedo attacks and to fight off enemy escorts. They are also used for independent actions such as scouting, raiding, protecting transports and chasing pirates.

SHIP CLASSES

The ships of the Imperial fleet are split into a number of classes. All ships in the same class are more or less identical in design, though many have been modified during refits, or as a result of damage suffered in battle.

SPACE MARINE BATTLE BARGES

Most Space Marine Chapters control a handful of Battle Barges. They are exceedingly brutal vessels, with only one purpose behind their design. As might be expected, a Battle Barge is configured for close support of planetary landings and carries numerous bombardment turrets and torpedo tubes. A considerable amount of hull space is given over to launch bays for intra-system craft and drop pods; most of these capital ships have a cavernous maw at their bows, from which Thunderhawk Gunships and other such craft can attack. All told, Battle Barges can deploy up to three companies simultaneously. These vessels are extremely heavily armoured and well shielded, so that they can breach planetary defences without harm coming to their cargo. Naturally, the Battle Barge makes a frightening opponent in any situation where boarding is involved.

IMPERIAL NAVY DICTATOR CLASS CRUISERS

Dictator class cruisers are built around Lunar class hulls, with the lance decks entirely replaced with launch bays for attack craft. This stop-gap measure was envisaged as a simple method of delivering large numbers of atmospheric craft, like Thunderbolt fighters and Marauder bombers, to low orbit, to support ground-based operations. However, successive upgrades to the Dictator's communications and detection systems expanded its capabilities for launching long-range strikes against ships in deep space. These attack craft carriers were increasingly equipped with Fury class deep space fighters and Starhawk bombers, and operated either as support vessels for battlefleets or as independent patrol ships throughout the Sector. A single Dictator with a handful of escort craft proved an exceedingly flexible force, capable of running down pirates and even raiding hostile worlds.

IMPERIAL NAVY SWORD CLASS FRIGATES

The venerable Sword class frigate has ably served the Imperial Navy for thousands of years. Every part of the vessel's design and construction has been tried and tested in innumerable engagements. The Sword's laser-based weapons batteries and substantial turret array have an exceptional ready level of 88.2%. Its plasma drives are simple, sturdy units copied many times on other ships and can be serviced by artificers with minimal training. A classic escort vessel in every respect, few battleships fight without at least a pair of the reliable Swords to guard their backs against enemy destroyers and attack craft.

CHAOS SPACE MARINE BATTLEFLEETS

'Like the great storm of the Heresy, the forces of the True Gods will descend upon the False Emperor's minions. The stars will tremble at their passage, the mighty armadas of the Warmaster will bring annihilation to a hundred worlds. Great shall be the slaughter, most pleasing shall be the flow of blood…'

Long ago, when the Emperor of Mankind led his Space Marine Legions across the stars in what was to become known as the Great Crusade, Primarchs captained his armies. Each Primarch commanded not only a Legion of Space Marines but also vast fleets of warships and innumerable armies of Guardsmen. The military might at the disposal of each of them was immense. Then came the Horus Heresy, when fully half the Primarchs rebelled against the Emperor. The history of the Heresy is well-known; it was a dark and terrible time in which civil war almost destroyed the Imperium. In its aftermath, it was clear to the High Lords that too much power had been at the disposal of the traitor Primarchs, and major reforms were made to the Space Marine Legions,

Of course, the defeated Traitor Legions were never a part of these Imperial reforms. When Guilliman wrote the Codex Astartes, effectively breaking the remaining loyal Legions down into smaller Chapters, the Black Legion, the World Eaters and all their fellow renegades were establishing empires in the Eye of Terror using all the forces they had salvaged from the defeat on Terra. To this day, many of the lords of the Chaos Space Marines control vast fleets of warships. The Traitor Legions have never needed to build specialist Battle Barges and Strike Cruisers, for the craft they have fought from since the days of the Heresy serve them still, their ancient hulls modified, embellished and repaired over and over until they show little sign their Imperial heritage.

However, Traitor Marines are rare figures of dark legend even within the Eye of Terror and a great many of the Chaos fleets that plague the Imperium are led by renegade captains, with not a Traitor Marine in sight. The degree of fealty these rogue captains extend to their Chaos Marine masters is variable; certainly, some pirate fleets that ostensibly serve Chaos have probably never seen a Chaos Space Marine, though this does not stop their ships and crews drawing the eye of the Dark Gods.

CHAOS DESPOILER CLASS BATTLESHIP

The Despoiler class battleships were developed as part of the Gareox Prerogative in the mid-36th millennium. A belief in the strength of attack craft as the ultimate weapons in space warfare pervaded the Battlefleet Tempestus and plans were made for fifteen Despoiler class battleships. However, as history shows, the true battleship was not outmoded by the ramping-up of attack craft use in fleet-on-fleet engagements, and the program was ended after the construction of just three vessels. The Despoilers originally saw little combat, being used on long-range patrols through largely uncontested systems. Roughly two hundred and fifty years after being laid down, the *Merciless Death* went missing whilst on extended tour through the Amerikon Sector. Thirty years later, it reappeared during the Banardi Conflict, surprising and destroying a convoy of sixteen unprotected Imperial transports en route to Banardi Prime. The ship was then involved in numerous engagements, each progressively nearer to the Eye of Terror, until it disappeared again in early M39. Soon after its second disappearance, the other two Despoilers in the Imperial Fleet were also reported absent, after firing on defenceless friendly vessels and then escaping into the Warp. With the advent of the Gothic War, rumours of the *Merciless Death's* exploits and sightings of its sister ships began afresh.

CHAOS REPULSIVE CLASS GRAND CRUISER

The grand cruiser was a precursor to the battlecruisers which are now more prevalent in most Imperial fleets. Almost rivalling battleships in its ability to withstand damage and lay down a barrage of fire, the grand cruiser design fell out of favour when the means for constructing sufficiently powerful engines were lost (those engines built more recently were incapable of attaining a useful combat speed for craft of this scale). A few ancient grand cruisers can still be found in service in the reserve fleets of the Segmentum Obscurus and Segmentum Pacificus, but as a whole the class is largely obsolete.

Of the twenty-five grand cruisers believed to have abandoned the Emperor since their inception in the 34th millennium, roughly a dozen have yet to be recaptured or destroyed. Of those still at large, the *Foe-Reaper* is the most active, having been sighted in more than a score of major fleet engagements in the twenty-three centuries since her corruption by the Dark Powers. Most infamously, it was the *Foe-Reaper* which destroyed the Adeptus Mechanicus facility on AFR-74, killing fifty thousand Adepts and Skitarii within a few heartbeats by firing a salvo of specially modified torpedoes which shattered the eco-shield protecting the inhabitants from the metha-nitrous atmosphere of that satellite.

CHAOS SLAUGHTER CLASS CRUISER

The Slaughter class cruiser utilises a scartix engine coil, that provides the ship with a thrust considerably more powerful than any other vessel's. When the *Dutiful*, a Slaughter class cruiser laid down in 126.M34, turned renegade and bombarded the Sethelan forge world, the design for the priceless scartix coil was destroyed, setting back the design and production of new Imperial vessels considerably. Some think the attack had the sole purpose of preventing the construction of any more Slaughter class vessels. The *Dutiful* was re-named the *Soulless* by Admiral Dorez for this despicable deed and was mercilessly hunted across Imperial space for the next seven millennia. It was finally destroyed during the Orar Raid, when its plasma drives were wrecked by the *Imperious*, a Mars class battlecruiser.

CHAOS IDOLATOR CLASS RAIDER

The Idolator class raider is something of an enigma. Little is known of the whereabouts of its construction, though it is rumoured they are built on the excommunicated forge world of Xana II near the Eye of Terror. Idolators incorporate many systems and features which are of obviously of non-human origin, probably bought or stolen from other space-faring races, such as Kroot mercenaries and Fra'al raiders. These escort-sized vessels show remarkable gunnery at long range and it is speculated that they benefit from some kind of improved targeting system which cannot be widely replicated by the Adeptus Mechanicus. Squadrons of Idolators are a constant menace to shipping near the Eye of Terror and it is not uncommon for three or four of these vessels to slip through the blockade of the Cadian Gate and wreak havoc on the vulnerable convoys serving Cadia before escaping back into the depths of the void, despite the best efforts of nearby Imperial defenders.

INDEX